Traumatic States

Traumatic States

Gendered Violence, Suffering,
and Care in Chile

Nia Parson

Vanderbilt University Press

NASHVILLE

© 2013 by Vanderbilt University Press
Nashville, Tennessee 37235
All rights reserved
First printing 2013

This book is printed on acid-free paper.
Manufactured in the United States of America

Library of Congress Cataloging-in-Publication Data on file

LC control number 2012030216
LC classification HV6626.23.C5P37 2013
Dewey class number 362.82'92 — dc23

ISBN 978–0-8265–1895–8 (cloth)
ISBN 978–0-8265–1897–2 (e-book)

For you, my dear Amelia

CONTENTS

ACKNOWLEDGMENTS

Since the first time I traveled to Santiago, Chile, in the southern hemisphere's winter of 2000 to conduct preliminary fieldwork, I have become indebted to so many people who helped me produce this book and who saw me through the process it took to arrive here. Though I will not be able to name each person who has contributed, for those who remain nameless here, as well as the ones whose support and encouragement I mention, thank you. Although this work would not have been possible without these individuals and the wide communities of which I am a part, any errors and omissions herein are, of course, mine.

As my mentors in the Rutgers University Department of Anthropology, Dorothy Hodgson and Peter Guarnaccia have provided me with consistent and valuable support and intellectually stimulating ideas for directions to take. Their scholarship has continued to be a beacon for my own career and to inspire me to push through to new and meaningful analyses. I was fortunate to work with Peter, first as a graduate student, then as a Postdoctoral Fellow in the Rutgers Institute for Health's National Institute for Mental Health Postdoctoral Program. He introduced me to the field of trauma and recovery and to examining categories for understanding people's many forms and manifestations of suffering. Dorothy encouraged me to think about women's agency and power in new ways. She consistently pushed me to improve my ability to express my ideas in written form with her incisive, challenging, and productive readings of my work. I have benefited greatly from Dorothy's skill and precision as an ethnographer.

Meredeth Turshen's insights into how wider suffering affects women's lives in particular ways have greatly influenced my thinking. Her passion for bringing to light how women's experiences of health and illness, and war and recovery are shaped by inequalities has accompanied me when it was difficult to continue. Her beautiful artwork has accompanied me as well. Charlotte Bunch's work on UN women's rights frameworks as director of the Center for Women's Global Leadership at Rutgers University greatly influenced my interest in and dedication to the topic of domestic violence against women as a human rights issue. In particular I am grateful for my involvement with the Women's Global Leadership Institute during the summer of 2002. Janet Siskind provided her generous support of my work and introduced me to Lesley Gill. I had the great fortune to know Lesley and receive her mentorship and learn from her scholarship. She pushed my thinking about gender, class, and militarization in Latin America and I learned so much from the conversations she, Andrew Bickford, and I shared around her kitchen table. I continue to draw from her work and the many insights and great energy she shared with me.

Southern Methodist University provided generous support for my follow-up research in 2009 and 2011 and for the writing of this book. I am also grateful for support from the Sam Taylor Foundation for my 2009 field trip to Chile. Writing of this book was also supported by a National Institute for Mental Health Postdoctoral Fellowship at the Rutgers University Institute for Health, where I had the opportunity to be mentored by Alan Horwitz, David Mechanic, and Peter Guarnaccia. I am grateful for the support I received to complete this research from 2002 to 2004 from the Fulbright-Hays program, the Wenner-Gren Foundation for Anthropological Research, and the Rutgers University Graduate School. Thank you especially to Teresa Del Corso at Rutgers, who provided me with thorough, critical, crucial, and patient readings of drafts of these grant proposals. I also received a Rutgers University Bevier Award to complete my dissertation write-up, as well as a Rutgers University Institute for Research on Women Fellowship for my participation in their seminar, "Diversity: Expanding Theory and Practice," during the 2004–2005 year.

Mostly, I owe a great debt to the women whose voices make this book speak and who made it possible for me to write this book. Without their participation and generosity in sharing their painful and tri-umphant stories with me, this book would not exist. For the women who suffered domestic violence in Chile who are my friends and those with whom I was in contact only for a brief moment, I hope that I have managed to do some justice here to their experiences and expressions. They taught me so much about their own lives and about life. I thank them for participating in this project and sharing intimate details of their life stories. Their courage was a constant source of inspiration as I wrote this book. I will not mention any of their names here because I am ethically bound to maintain their anonymity in all ways possible, but I will use the pseudonyms for the women whose stories most loudly inform my analysis. *Gracias, Marisol. Eres una amiga para siempre y me das mucha energía para seguir luchando. Gracias, Luz, por darme la oportunidad de aprender de ti sobre como crecer a través de la pena. Gracias, Josefina, por compartir tus experiencias tan profundas.*

The various staff members at Safe Space and the director and staff at Family Care were always supportive and more than generous in wel-coming me into their professional worlds. I am in their debt for having taught me so much about their work and the contexts in which they help women who suffer domestic violence. Many thanks to Chilean sociologist Carolina Soto for her support of my work and for her kind friendship. *Quiero darle las gracias a mi querida amiga, Xime.* My most heartfelt gratitude goes to Xime, whose insights are so coherent and whose life work toward improving women's rights is truly exemplary and a source of reflection and motivation.

My participation in the 2004–2005 Rutgers University Institute for Research on Women Seminar nourished my thinking. The scholarship and ideas that abounded in the weekly seminars were inspirational. I especially appreciated Nancy Hewitt's mentorship and her support of my scholarship, and Temma Kaplan's pointed advice on my project pushed me to delve deeper into feminist historical analyses of the Chil-ean historical context.

Chapter 6 is based on my article entitled, "Transformative Ties: Gendered Violence, Forms of Recovery, and Shifting Subjectivities in Chile," published in the journal *Medical Anthropology Quarterly*, pro-duced by the American Anthropological Association, and I am grateful to reproduce some of that here. I also thank Mark Luborsky, as well as the anonymous reviewers, for a very productive set of exchanges that helped me to refine my analysis in that article.

Many friends have been supportive along the way. I thank Molly Burke-León for the many conversations we shared over the years about our mutual interests in women's lives, stories, and gender equality. Thank you to Meg Winnecour, who is a great inspiration and creative spirit and who translated this book into the painting that graces its cover. Mylene Labrin's friendship, sharp wit, and practical support helped me to navigate my first visits to Chile and well beyond. Mylene, you are one of my personal heroes, as you know. Thank you for my smart, brave, and kind Emilio and Pascal. Family members in Chile have been consistently a source of support. Thank you Nona, Carlos, Sandra, Claudio, Noah, Simón, Carlos Andrés, Nico, Violeta, Mario, Jimena, Sofía, Gabriel, and Matías. I consider Nancy Noton, Manuel Echeverría, and their family an important part of our Chilean family who offer us constant warmth and friendship.

Other friends and colleagues have influenced my thinking and provided support at pivotal moments and for them I am eternally grateful: Hillary Haldane, Madelaine Adelman, Cristina Alcalde, Lynn Kwiatkowski, Srimati Basu, Jennifer Wies, Jane Henrici, Richard Schroeder, Lisa Vanderlinden, Mona Bhan, Noelle Molé, Robert Marlin, Rebecca Etz, Anita Figueroa, Marcelo Coddou, Claudia Cabello, Felipe Troncoso, Susan Dixon, Arpita Chakrabarty, and Andrew Bickford. Peggy Barlett, Peter Brown, and George Armelagos, professors I was privileged to receive tutelage from during my undergraduate career at Emory University, spurred and have supported my endeavors to contribute to the production of anthropological knowledges. I am also grateful to Claire Renzetti, who has given me immense intellectual support as well as feminist mentorship. At SMU colleagues in various positions have supported my scholarship: Beth Newman, Sheri Kunovich, Evelyn Parker, Rick Halphin, Kathleen Hugley-Cook, Renee MacDonald, Ernie Jouriles, and LaiYee Leong and Jeffrey Kahn (and their daughter, Sophia Kahn). Special thanks to William Tsutsui, dean of Dedman College, for his support of my ongoing research, scholarly interests, and professional development and for the incredible intellectual energy he brings to SMU.

This book is also for my parents, Nancy Nolte Parson and Jack Parson, who always encouraged me to pursue my intellectual interests and supported me in those pursuits in so many ways. Their devotion to lifelong curiosity and learning play an important role in propelling me forward in my own quests to greater understanding and to explore new places and ideas. I am lucky to have a father who is also an academic and who read and offered such crucial comments on drafts of my manuscript. Special thanks to Jack Parson for your mentorship and for your close readings of and productive conversations about this book as it progressed. I am also so grateful for my brother, Daniel Parson, for my sister-in-law, Molly McGehee, and for my nephew Benjamin Parson. This book is also for my grandmothers, Dorothy Basinger Parson and Ethel Hackman Nolte, brave women who blazed important pathways toward a better world, each in her own way.

At Southern Methodist University I have been lucky to work within a remarkably supportive and critically engaged scholarly environment. I am extremely grateful to have Caroline Brettell as a scholarly beacon. Caroline's intellectual acumen, theoretical sophistication and passion for ethnographic engagement, skilled leadership, great wisdom, generosity, and support make her, her life, and her work a constant example for me. I am most grateful for Carolyn Smith-Morris's constant and many forms of support and mentorship since I have been at SMU. Carolyn's passion for medical anthropology is one of the reasons the field will continue to move forward in the vibrant forms it is taking. Her attention to the ways that medical anthropologists can make interdisciplinary links with clinicians and practitioners in medical fields and her devotion to understanding people's lives in local contexts are exemplary of what medical anthropology can be. I am fortunate to have Victoria Lockwood as a friend and colleague at SMU. Victoria has provided me with extraordinary support and I have learned so much from her expertise in methods. She and I have shared productive and enlightening conversations about our shared research interests in intimate partner violence. In 2010 we, along with Cristina Alcalde and Lynn Kwiatkowski, co-organized an executive session for the 2010

American Anthropological Association Conference in New Orleans, entitled "The Impacts of Global Circulations on Gendered Violence." I had the great fortune to count Sarah Willen as a colleague at SMU for two years. She is truly an admirable colleague who gracefully manages both theoretical sophistication and active engagement with issues around undocumented migration and health. I am also most grateful to Robert Van Kemper and Ben Wallace for their support and for their roles as models for maintaining a lifetime of vibrant scholarship. For the years this book was under completion, I was privileged to have David Meltzer as my department chair. His sage advice and his sharp wit are always thoughtful and much appreciated, as has been his support of my research and scholarship. Thank you for all you do for all of us, Pamela Hogan and Tiffany Powell. You make the SMU Anthropology Department run. Several SMU doctoral students have contributed in various ways to this book. Thank you in particular to Carina Heckert, Megan Bond Hinrichsen, Jessica Lott, Saira Mehmood, Amber Zabka, Shay Cannedy, and Faith Nibbs.

I am eternally grateful for the intellectual mentorship João Biehl provided me at a crucial moment when I assisted him with his course, Medical Anthropology, at Princeton University during the 2008–2009 academic year. João opened up such important intellectual avenues and possibilities for me, as a scholar and as a teacher, as he has done for so many others. His vision for anthropology in general and medical anthropology in particular has been and will continue to be a constant inspiration in my career. Thank you as well to the Princeton University Department of Anthropology for the opportunity to teach there. I also thank Rayna Rapp, Fred Myers, and Bambi Schiefflin at New York University's Department of Anthropology for their support during the 2008–2009 academic year when I had the opportunity to teach Medical Anthropology and Anthropology of Gender there. I am grateful to Sally Engle Merry, also at NYU's Department of Anthropology, for sharing with me some of her expertise and introducing me to her work on global governance. Her scholarship on gender violence is groundbreaking and foundational for many of us who are scholars of gender violence. I am grateful to Mindie Lazarus-Black, whose scholarship on domestic violence and the law in Trinidad influenced my thinking greatly. In particular I am grateful for her comments during a panel that I organized entitled "Intimate Violence, Global Migration, Suffering and Survival" for the 2008 American Anthropological Association Annual Meeting in San Francisco.

I owe an enormous intellectual debt to Hillary Haldane, one of the leading anthropological scholars of gender-based violence who reviewed this book and did so thoughtfully, carefully, and generously. Hillary's comments helped me to rework the manuscript's theoretical thrust substantially, and she encouraged me to foreground Luz's, Marisol's, and Josefina's narratives and voices more loudly and strongly. Thank you, Hillary. I also have enduring gratitude for Madelaine Adelman's incisive and thorough review of my manuscript at crucial junctures and for her critical suggestions for how to further develop and highlight theoretical points and my own voice as a feminist scholar throughout the book. Thank you, Madelaine. Enormous thanks go as well to Eli Bortz at Vanderbilt University Press, with whom I worked most closely and who saw the reviews of the manuscript through the process seamlessly and efficiently. I am so grateful for Michael Ames's interest in this project, which he expressed from the time that Peter Guarnaccia so generously introduced me to him at the Society for Medical Anthropology's conference, "Medical Anthropology at the Intersections," at Yale University in 2009. I am also most grateful to the talented production editor, Dariel Mayer, at Vanderbilt University Press, who made crucial revisions to the manuscript and contributed so much to this project through her attention to detail in various dimensions of the production process.

Lastly, I will always be grateful to Pablo Mora, who saw me through this project, from its inception and through all of its phases, with his unswerving support, gifted intellect, clear vision, and persistence, not to mention his constant attention to mundane yet all-important household tasks and raising our brave daughter, Amelia Mora-Parson, the love of our lives.

Traumatic States

PROLOGUE

That wound is open until the end. That's what
he's done to me. —Josefina, in 2003

In so far as the past is felt to continually reenter the present,
time is synchronous. —Michael Jackson (2010:139)

Life after Death

On a late afternoon in the early fall of 2002 Luz stumbled her way
from her house in a suburb of Santiago to a nearby street corner, her
chest bathed in blood, a bullet lodged in her chest. Her husband
had shot her at point-blank range in their bedroom, almost mortally
wounding her. The doctors told her later that her survival was miracu-
lous. "I wasn't living," Luz told me about her twenty-five-year marriage
to her husband, as we talked over coffee in a bustling downtown Santiago café in 2009. Luz felt that her life had revolved around trying to
be a good wife, a good mother, a good woman. "Chilean women are
too good," she mused. By 2009, Luz was living her life after death and
recovering herself after years of abuse and repression. Her husband was
dead from a self-inflicted gunshot fired directly after he attempted to
murder Luz.

So many women have suffered.

Bruises, broken arms, broken ribs, bloody noses, knife wounds,
scarred faces, gunshot wounds, burns, coma, paralysis, loss of language, depression, anxiety, brain damage, rape, damaged vaginas, sexually transmitted diseases, gushing blood, hopelessness, near-death.
Purchasing himself a car and neglecting her sore tooth, using her hard-
earned money to buy drugs, telling her she is a slut and a whore, telling

her that without him she would die because he provides the food, constantly surveilling her every move. *Pain.*

In 1991, the first-ever study of domestic violence in Chile confirmed that in Santiago, the capital of about five million people, 60 percent of women had suffered some form of domestic violence in their lifetimes.[1] In 2002, another study confirmed the magnitude and widespread nature of women's suffering, with 50 percent of women reporting that they had suffered domestic violence.[2] The problem once thought of as limited to the intimate sphere of the family and interpersonal relationships between men and women had only recently been named "domestic violence" and called into question by the feminist movement in Chile, as it has been globally. The numbers now highlighted what many women had already lived in obscurity. The abuses and suffering are entrenched. In 2002 Luz almost became one of a multitude of women murdered by their intimate partners, but she survived to tell her story and to live again.[3]

Yet numbers paint a sterile picture, obscuring the broken limbs, the broken lives, the ruptured and diminished selves. They distract the vision from women's active and continuous struggles for life after death, for recoveries in their many forms. I listened, with an ethnographer's ear, to stories of women, like Luz, who had suffered such abuse, and paid close attention to the effects of various forms of violence on their bodies, minds, and senses of self. Pain is written onto and into their embodied minds and mindful bodies, but this is only part of the story they tell.

Dead in Life: Patti

Patti and I met twice in 2003 in a large and warm room, surrounded by a beautifully maintained garden full of fruit trees. The room was often used for group therapy sessions at Safe Space, a nongovernmental organization (NGO) dedicated to women's rights and to addressing domestic violence in particular. As we walked there I noted that Patti had some difficulty moving her legs and walked in an awkward way, as though her feet didn't move as she wanted. In one of her arms she clutched a magazine close to her chest. She explained to me that it had been seven years since she had suddenly become "sick."

"I was in very bad shape, in intensive care . . . in a coma. . . . Everyone thought that I was going to go. They told my husband: 'Unfortunately, your wife will not make it through the night. And if she does, she will be a vegetable.'"

Patti smiled and told me, "So, I'm a miracle of God. . . . A real living miracle."

"Do you remember being in the hospital?" I asked, wanting to understand more about her experiences and memories of that time.

"Everyone came to see me when I was in the hospital. I was full of machines, full of machines. Machines were everywhere," she remembered. "I couldn't talk. I didn't control my sphincter. They bandaged my eyes because I was left without vision."

Her bodily integrity had been violated completely. Could it really have been her husband who damaged her so wholly? I suspected it but still did not know how to ask.

"I am alive," she told me. "Before, I was dead. I was in a coma. But in reality I was dead in life."

Patti spent one month in the hospital. "But for me," she said, "it felt like twenty years."

Her loss of control over her body and her life were total in the hospital.

"All the time the nurses come to change you. Wash you. Cut your hair," she told me. "My hair was long. They cut it. They washed it with whatever kind of shampoo. All my life I took care of it with a special shampoo, and it wasn't the same. It wasn't the way you did things in your own house."

"Day and night they injected me," she remembered. "They took blood. . . . I had hoses, was full of machines. They took me to do X-rays. All day they took me here and there in my cot. It was terrible."

After Patti had voluntarily shared many painful memories with me, I finally wondered aloud whether she knew when she awoke from her coma in the hospital how she had become "sick."

"No, I didn't know," she said. "The only thing that I knew was that there were nurses, that I was hospitalized. . . . The first time I saw my husband I didn't think that he had hurt me like this. . . . Later, when I returned to my house . . . I started to remember [the violence]."

"My husband asked for my forgiveness because I still wasn't talking," she told me. "He asked for my forgiveness, and then I remembered what had happened. He beat me. He beat me savagely. He beat me in a very brutal and ugly way. From those beatings I have this sickness," Patti told me, seemingly at peace with this revelation.

"And when you left the hospital, I imagine that whole time period was very difficult for you," I offered.

"I was so submerged in that hole, I thought that I was going to die," she replied. "I'm talking about after I had left the hospital, I had a very terrible depression, day and night, depression, when the only thing you want is to die. I remembered. I wanted to die."

During that time, she said, "I cried, cried, cried. Nobody could make me feel better. And now I talk. I don't cry. . . . I don't have that oppression here anymore. I didn't talk. I cried. I didn't talk. Incredible."

Patti had been reduced in many ways to a state of infancy, a state of total dependence on others.

"I couldn't move. They left me in my house in a cot. I couldn't even move my neck. My neck fell over onto itself. I couldn't hold up my head because it would fall backwards. Nothing. I couldn't see. I didn't talk. . . . They sat me up and I fell backwards. They had to tie me up. Yes, it's incredible."

"I used a cane for many years," she said. "I didn't leave the cane even to go to the bathroom."

"My husband taught me how to talk because I wasn't able to say anything. I started with 'a,' 'e,' 'pa,' 'pe,' all of the letters, the same as when I was a baby . . . a little kid."

Paralysis: Marisol

Marisol and I sat in her living room in 2003, her daughter upstairs studying, her beloved dog on the back porch, her kitten, Plata, cuddled up next to me on the couch, as she began to tell her story to me, a stranger made instantly known through an introduction from Ema, the Safe Space staff member who made my research there possible.

"I got married to a person I didn't know," Marisol began. "I didn't know how he was as a person."

"Socially he didn't let me develop myself as a woman. I didn't have the right to a sex life. I didn't have the right to express my desires, my dreams. . . . I think that his biggest fight was against my dreams. Against the dreams that I had. He took all of that away—my economic freedom, my social freedom, to dream, to develop my life's project."

"My life's project was truncated," she said painfully. "But still, I don't consider myself to be a woman who is a failure, not at all, because I say, 'I fought with the tools that I had, did what I could.'"

"[Soon] I started to develop sicknesses," Marisol told me. "One starts to develop real and psychosomatic sicknesses. I was so paralyzed by the violence. I was so sick, not only psychologically, but also physically. I stopped walking. I arrived at that extreme."

Gerardo, her abusive husband, took her to a psychiatrist. She recalls telling the psychiatrist that he "didn't treat me like a woman, he treated me like a girl. . . . In our everyday interactions, he treated me like a girl. *And I wasn't a girl.* I was a twenty-seven-year-old woman."

Marisol felt the psychiatrist discounted her suffering because he found Gerardo to be charming, a smooth talker.

On the other hand, the gynecologist who treated her repeatedly for her "sicknesses," as she referred to the sexually transmitted diseases she often suffered, offered to help her escape to her parents' home in the south by writing a medical order to that effect.

"And I hadn't told him anything," Marisol remembered. "But he knew. He understood, of course, because of his experience and profession."

"And now, lately," she continued, "I have been remembering things that one keeps inside, that one wants to forget."

Her recent pap smear for cervical cancer had come out badly.

"They called me from the clinic, [and said] that I had [possible signs of] uterine cancer. . . . I went to the hospital to have more tests, and they asked me even more intimate questions," she said.

"And I began to remember that this wasn't the first time the exams had come out badly, and I had to have a lot of cauterizations. It was because of the infections he gave me," she told me sadly. "The truth is that none of the treatments were well done," she lamented.

"I never had a break [from the diseases]. Now I'm ready to confront what will happen, but I'm very worried about my daughters. . . . I'm very angry," Marisol told me.

Then she explained to me why she did not "deserve" the lack of care Gerardo had shown her. After all, she protested, she had been a "good woman" to him.

"Although I'm not a perfect woman," she said, "I always tried to be the best woman for him in every way. I always learned about sex, the best for him. But anyway, he never recognized this at all."

For Marisol, the STDs were an embodied reminder of Gerardo's lack of care for her, his abuse of her body and mind.

"It makes me very angry and makes me embarrassed," she lamented.

Though it was not easy for her to divulge these details to me, part of Marisol's self-defined "leitmotif" was to share her experiences of abuse so that other women could learn.

When I visited Marisol again, during the winter of 2009, this time near the Chilean coast about two hours from Santiago where she was then living with her youngest daughter, she explained some of the desperation she had been feeling since Gerardo had returned from Argentina to occupy the house where she lived until his return in 2006. Marisol could not bear to live with him and since his return she had felt forced to move around among her mother's, sister's, and daughter's homes in different regions of Chile.

"It's painful," she said. "It's paralyzing. Living violence is very paralyzing. It's like you think, 'I don't have rights. There's no one above me who can help me. And where is this God? This God, who they say is good and doesn't punish?'"

She rejected the idea that somehow it was her fault that she had suffered Gerardo's abuses: "Many say, 'This is your karma. This is the life you chose.' What do I have to do with this 'karma'?" she asked, rhetorically.

Marisol's health problems continued, unabated, over time. Sitting at her small, neat dining table in her living room in 2009, Marisol explained to me that the stroke she had suffered in 2007 was also related to her husband's ongoing violence against her. Her doctors had a more individualistic, biologically oriented perspective.

"After the stroke," she said, "They all told me, 'Of course, it's high blood pressure.'"

"Right," she protested to me, "but you have to know what the causes of the high pressure were. That is very important. I have done my analyses, and I know what caused the elevation in my blood pressure."

It seemed that she had been over this in her mind many times before.

"It dawned on me that my family had fallen apart, my space, my rights, everything. When [my daughter] was going to visit [from Germany, with her new husband], it was like I saw the truth," she explained. *"I could fully grasp the real dimensions of the consequences of the violence."*

She had no place for her daughter and new son-in-law to stay, no home of her own where she could receive them, because Gerardo had claimed their house as his own.

According to Marisol, the consequences of Gerardo's abuses continued to manifest in her physical and psychological ailments, which added to the health problems caused by her lifelong genetic disorder.

"My body is tired," she said. "It is difficult to move around. It's hard for me to walk. My feet hurt a lot. I'm waiting for the surgeon to see me because they told me that I have internal varicose veins, which also can cause a lot of pain."

She also suffered from incontinence due to the stroke and was on a waiting list for an operation, "to improve my quality of life," she said.

"I heal myself because of self-love," she insisted in 2009, even in the face of her mounting infirmities and lack of her own home.

I Haven't Lived at All: Josefina

Josefina's mother abandoned her soon after she was born, relinquishing her to family members and adoptive parents. Josefina was a tender twelve years old when her adoptive parents arranged her marriage to a twenty-three-year-old man to whom she still remained married thirty-five years later, when I met her at Family Care in 2003. On their wedding night, she said, he raped her and then accused her of being *una puta* (a whore). Almost immediately Josefina became pregnant with their first child and soon after had a second.

"He only created them," Josefina told me as we sat in one of the therapy offices upstairs at Family Care in 2003.

"He treated me badly. He humiliated me every chance he got. Never came out of his mouth a word of affection. A lifetime crying. A lifetime suffering. A lifetime being enslaved to a man," she said to me to express the emotional damage she felt.

"In the mornings many people thank God for living another day," she told me painfully. "But I say, 'Why didn't you take me while I was sleeping last night, God?' . . . My intention isn't to live."

"I am very childish," Josefina lamented. "I can't resign myself to the fact that I am an adult person. Yes, that is the terrible thing."

"And that I haven't lived at all."

CHAPTER I

Unfinished Care

How can the anthropological artifact keep the story
moving and unfinished? —João Biehl (2005:24)

Behind the powerlessness of God peeps the powerlessness
of man [i.e., humans], who continues to cry, "May that
never happen again!" When it is clear that "that" is by
now, everywhere. —Giorgio Agamben (1999:20)

A single traumatic event can occur almost anywhere.
Prolonged, repeated trauma, by contrast, occurs only
in circumstances of captivity [such as] in prisons,
concentration camps, and slave labor camps . . .
and in families. —Judith Herman (1992:74)

Suffering and Healing: Making the Invisible Visible

The experiences of Luz, Marisol, Josefina, and other women highlight
various types of violence, care-seeking, and continual processes of recovering some aspects of a life after death. This book shows how Luz,
Marisol, and Josefina, in particular, are continually reordering their
senses of themselves in the never-ending present as they review wounds
of the past in light of the present and in terms of their perceptions of
future possibilities. The emergence of domestic violence as an object
of state intervention in the late 1980s and early 1990s in Chile brought
novel possibilities for women to engage in processes of naming, care
seeking, and working through the pain and suffering caused by domestic violence. Before, domestic violence had in many ways been seen
as merely a "normal" part of the social fabric, and the power inequalities that made this form of violence against women possible remained

9

largely "invisible" (Kleinman, Das, and Lock 1997a:xiii).[1] Though violence was not entirely invisible to the women who suffered it or others who knew about it, it was invisible in the sense that it was seen simply as "the way things are."[2]

The "invisibility" of domestic violence against women and the suffering it entails are related to the difficulty of communicating the pain of being subject to violence by an intimate partner and to the challenges of being truly heard in that communication. The many forms of violence—physical, sexual, emotional, psychological, economic, and social—that are main features of an abusive domestic relationship are in essence an attempt at the "conversion of absolute pain into the fiction of absolute power" (Scarry 1985:27). Pain destroys language, but sometimes language to describe forms of pain simply does not exist, and the failure to speak pain can have dire consequences (14).[3] Without the ability to express pain, violence and the power inequalities that produce it can remain obscured. The ability to express pain requires language for talking about the pain, identification of the origins of the pain, and the willingness and ability of individuals and institutions to hear that pain and address it, to shift power relations in such a way as to rework the sources of the pain. Since the 1970s in some parts of the world and since the late 1980s in Chile, language has evolved to express that suffering and bring the invisible into view.

Traumatic States illuminates how Marisol, Luz, and Josefina have experienced the effects of the state's new attention to women's gendered suffering in Chile, showing how their intimate, lived experiences intersect with wider political and economic processes (see Biehl 2005).[4] My critical phenomenological approach sheds light on entanglements among macro-level, biopolitical structures and micro-level subjectivities and shows how wider processes and in particular state formations and transformations coalesce in individuals' lived experiences. Humans live socially, in relationship with others. Even abandonment and isolation, seemingly asocial phenomena, are deeply social and socially produced (see Biehl 2005). Suffering is lived in the mindful bodies and embodied minds of individuals, and those individuals are inextricably bound in webs of relationships to others, both near and far.[5] By looking closely at the lives of Luz, Marisol, and Josefina, we can see how this interrelatedness goes beyond individual and family relationships, extending to market and state structures and to policies and practices at local and global levels. Subjectivities are forged in relationship with other people but importantly are also formed in interactions with bureaucracies of the state and its legal structures.

Power dynamics are central to women's gendered suffering, and power relationships are intimately social. Violence is about the will to power and control over other human beings, groups, situations, and resources. And, crucially, as Hannah Arendt points out in her 1970 book *On Violence*, "*Power* corresponds to the human ability not just to act but to act in concert. Power is never the property of an individual; it belongs to a group and remains in existence only so long as the group keeps together" (cited in Scheper-Hughes and Bourgois 2004:239). Domestic violence against women is lived in isolation and intimacy. However—and this is a crucial point—it is collective experience. The cross-cultural record demonstrates the collective nature of particular forms of gender-based violence against women (García-Moreno 2006). Historically, power inequalities that have disadvantaged women have been codified in the laws of states, and only in the past two decades has this been shifting in Chile.

Global Health and Domestic Violence

Domestic violence against women is a global health problem, with health defined as a state of complete well-being, not only as the absence of disease.[6] The World Health Organization Multi-Country Study on Violence against Women confirmed high rates of domestic violence in many countries throughout the world, as well as the cross-cultural negative mental and physical effects of this violence (García-Moreno 2006).[7] Physical death and also social death are risks for women who suffer domestic violence.[8] To assert that intimate partner violence against women is a public health problem is a true reflection of how such violence, along with other forms of violence against women, harms health and well-being. The health problems caused by intimate partner violence are certainly experienced by individuals. However, this means neither that causes and forms of care are located solely in individual bodies nor that the harm can be easily addressed by "magic bullet" biomedical and psychotherapeutic approaches. There are no "biotechnological embraces" (DelVecchio Good 2007) that will "fix" the problem and take away the memories of pain or medicate the ongoing struggles women face. This is because the violence, the material and psychological subjugation, and the attendant suffering are rooted in social ills, not in individual bodies and minds, though that is where the suffering and violence are made manifest. It is important to note that a public health approach to domestic violence is productive when it illuminates power structures that undergird the suffering produced by this form of violence.[9] In order to care for women who have suffered domestic violence, the social etiologies of their suffering need to be unwound (Kleinman et al. 1997b).

The more that the complicated roots of social suffering are examined through ethnography, the more those roots can be untangled. In the process of this disentanglement other pressing questions emerge: What is "recovery"? What does it mean to "heal" from domestic violence? The life history narratives of Marisol, Luz, and Josefina, embedded within deep ethnographic exploration of the contexts in which they were constructed, suggest that recoveries are ongoing and that healing is contingent and never complete. Healing is a process. Care is a process.

State and Intimate Violence, Families, and the Democracy-Era Legislation of Care

The lives of Marisol, Josefina, Luz, and other women who suffered domestic violence during the 2000s, their suffering and struggles, unfolded at a particular historical moment. The Chilean state was transitioning from a violent, repressive dictatorship to democratic governance, beginning in 1990, when the seventeen-year-long dictatorship ended. Throughout the dictatorial regime the state used various forms of violence, as well as the constant threat of violence, to suppress a culture of rights. Ideologies of "the family," defined as the nuclear, heterosexual family, intensified under the dictatorial regime and became a particularly important locus of the state's project of social control. Pinochet led the 1973 coup that toppled the democratically elected, socialist president Salvador Allende. Under Allende's "Chilean Road to Socialism," according to the dictatorial regime, "Chileans had 'lost their respect for authority,'" and Augusto Pinochet's government sought to restore this "respect" in part by promoting the image of an authoritarian family structure based in rigid gender roles and expectations. The woman was to be wife and mother, dutifully performing her nurturing *abnegada* (self-sacrificing, selfless woman) role, and the man was to assume the role of provider and authority figure (Trumper and Tomic 1998:4).[10] Under Pinochet, the Chilean nation was to be imagined as the "suprafamily" with Pinochet the authoritarian head whose "responsibility" it was to rein in the chaos caused by the "cancer of communism" unleashed by Allende's socialist government. All other families were to be based on this national imaginary, which sanctioned the use of violence to attain its ostensible goal of "order in the nation" (see Dandavati 2005; Htun 2003). Consider Pinochet's statement:

> When the social body sickens . . . it is not possible to enjoy every human right simultaneously. The immense majority of our fellow citizens accept and support [restrictions to human rights], because they understand that those restrictions are the price that has to be paid for tranquility, calm, and social peace, which today make us into an island within a world invaded by violence, terrorism, and generalized disorder. . . . When authority is not applied vigorously, we fall into depravity and after that into anarchy. (cited in Dorfman 2002:117–18)

In this formulation, the 2,279 people murdered by the state constituted a means to an end.[11] Their bodies were deemed disposable in order for the state to maintain "order" in the body politic—in the national family. During that time, actual families were deprived of information about how to find their disappeared members, and they sometimes resorted to often-futile letters of appeal to the authorities (see Morales 2000). Information continues to emerge regarding the true whereabouts of some victims' remains.

Many thousands of other men and women, including pregnant women, were tortured in state-run centers such as Villa Grimaldi in Santiago, where I visited with Luz and others in 2003 (see Rojas 2002).[12] Women who were political subversives were punished by the state not only for their antidictatorship activism but they were also punished for subverting dominant gender roles by acting against the interests of the "national family." In response, the torture inflicted on women specifically targeted their roles as mothers, wives, and nurturers and included various forms of rape (see Turshen 2000; Enloe 2000).[13] The violation and deep invasion of women's bodies was necessary, according to the state, for purposes of "national security." In turn, torture for men was often aimed at their masculinity, defined in terms of their relationships to women, and emphasized a man's helplessness to protect the bodies and sexualities of his female family members, lovers, and friends (Bunster-Burotto 1986:306).

The state thus legitimized intimate violence as a means of control over the "national family." Acts of direct state violence (see Agger and Jensen 1996), such as those that took place at the torture center Villa Grimaldi, were instances in which the state overtly intervened in its citizens' most intimate spaces, the most fundamental grounds of their existence, at once material and symbolic (Csordas 1990).[14] Mindful bodies, to invoke Scheper-Hughes and Lock's (1987) critique of the mind-body split in Western Enlightenment thought, were raped, mutilated, and shocked. Embodied minds were probed, manipulated, and tortured, often with lasting effects. Many of the women I interviewed had family members who had been tortured by, harassed by, or worked for the dictatorial state. The intensively violent incursions of the state into the intimate physical and mental spaces of its citizens during the era of the dictatorship constituted the most blatantly violent manifestation of the state's disciplinary interventions into its citizens' private lives (Foucault 1979).[15]

Lucia Hiriart de Pinochet, the dictator's wife, was also instrumental in promoting a particular version of state-sanctioned femininity during his regime. At the inauguration of the United Nations International Women's Year in 1975 she proclaimed, "The Chilean woman has understood how to achieve her duties, reestablishing in the soul of the people her role as a mother, the feeling of nationality, and faith in the destiny of our Fatherland" (Geis 1989, p. x). Hiriart de Pinochet was at the helm of the National Women's Agency and the mothers' centers.[16] In 1979 the government's Office of Planning (ODEPLAN) released a telling publication, which stated, "It should be kept in mind that every threat to the integrity of the family seriously affects the quality and quantity of the population, pathologically reducing the number of inhabitants and their integral formation. It has been proven that the birth rate decreases substantially with the disintegration of the family and increases with family stability. An affectionate, stable family life is the best environment for the development of children" (cited in Valdés 1991:100). Women were responsible for maintaining the nuclear family, which would produce many new citizens for the state. This family was integral to the state's formation during Pinochet's regime, and, thus, the state's intervention into intimate relationships was a matter of "national security." Seen in this light, the state's recent policies on domestic violence in the postdictatorship era constitute a novel manifestation of the state's historically gendered interventions into intimate relationships.

The neoliberal model was instituted in this violent and repressive context by "los Chicago Boys," Chilean economists who had been trained in the United States by Milton Friedman. Under the neoliberal economic model, imposed throughout the region and now heavily entrenched globally, the state's responsibility for social welfare shrinks and privatization expands. Citizens become, according to Aiwha Ong (2006:14), "free, self-managing, and self-enterprising individuals in different spheres of everyday life—health, education, bureaucracy, the professions. . . . The neoliberal subject is therefore not a citizen with claims on the state but a self-enterprising citizen-subject. . . . There is a new stress on responsibility at the community level, and new requirements that individual subjects be responsible for themselves." This neoliberal ethic and the political and economic structures built up around it constitute some of the most lasting traces of the dictatorship. Because of its exemplary neoliberal economy, Chile has earned the title of "South American Jaguar," though Chile was reported in 2011 to be the country with the highest level of income inequality among the thirty-four member states of the Organisation for Economic Co-operation and Development (Organisation for Economic Co-operation and Development 2011) and consistently ranks as one of the countries in the world with the highest levels of inequality between rich and poor.

The waning days of Pinochet's military dictatorship and the state's transition to an official democracy presented the possibility of making new demands for women's rights on the state. In particular, the women's rights movement was a major force in protesting the continuation of the dictatorship. They linked their demands for citizenship rights under democratic governance to women's right to be free from violence in their own homes, positing that women needed "Democracy in the Country and in the Home." In a 1988 plebiscite, Chileans voted against more years of Pinochet at the helm, signaling the official transformation of the state from one based on authoritarian rule to one based on democratic governance. Feminists formed the Women's Coalition for Democracy (Concertación de Mujeres por la Democracia) and forced women's rights to center stage throughout the official political transition to democracy (see Valenzuela, Gaviola, Largo, and Palestro 1994; Guillaudat and Mouterde 1998; Lúnecken Reyes 2000). The Women's Coalition for Democracy argued for women's full equality and promoted women's political participation in the nascent but still repressed civil society of the postdictatorship era (see Kaplan 2004). New forms of care for women who suffered domestic violence were central to their demands, as they positioned women's rights within the family as central to bringing democracy back to the country. In *Threads for a New Destination*, the Women's Coalition for Democracy outlined their goals for the gendered reform of the state in this transitional moment: "Power relationships inside the family have politico-social reach. An authoritarian family is a bad lesson for life in a democracy; moreover, it is difficult for women to effectively integrate themselves into political life while they remain in authoritarian ways of thinking inside the family. It is necessary for the home to be participative, for the family to democratize. It is indispensable to have a major dialogue between spaces of everyday life and politics" (Montecino Aguirre and Rossetti 1990:140). The coalition successfully pushed gender equality demands into state reforms in a variety of ways. In 1991 the Chilean government officially created the National

Women's Service (Servicio Nacional de la Mujer, known as SER-NAM), a subministerial entity charged with overseeing the implementation of gender equality throughout the state's policies and practices (Richards 2004). Domestic violence in particular became a major part of SERNAM's agenda and a key object of public policy. The passage of the first version of the Chilean Family Violence Law (Ley de Violencia Intrafamiliar No. 19.325) by the Chilean congress in 1994 (Gobierno de Chile 1994; see also SERNAM 2004b) was a landmark accomplishment for the feminist movement and for SERNAM. It was a remarkable reform, especially given the fragility of the official democracy in those years. Chile was one of the first countries in the region to pass a domestic violence law, and it did so within the context of a "global feminist consensus" on gender violence as a crucial issue (Johnson 2009). The 1994 Family Violence Law was passed at nearly the same time as the findings of the Chilean Truth and Reconciliation Commission (Rettig 1993) were made public, and policies to address both public and private violations of human rights have continuously developed since (Public prosecutors, personal interview, June 2009). In large part, the Chilean women's movement made this revolutionary moment for women's rights happen, within a very particular historical moment of global attention to women's rights and violence against women, and in concert with the Chilean state's modernization and redemocratization processes.

Although the first family violence law was a triumph for the feminist movement and SERNAM, from the moment of its passage many legislators, NGOs, and others were dissatisfied with aspects of it and worked consistently toward reforming its mechanisms (see Casas, Dides, and Perez 2001; El Agua Consultores Asociados 1997; Moltedo 1999). In many ways the 1994 Family Violence Law reinstated historically rooted ideals of the family and the place of women and men within it. The law encouraged "reconciliation" and sought to bolster the unity of "the family," the same ideological and patriarchal construction of "the family" that had always been figured as the "nucleus" of the Chilean nation. As the Chilean Police Training Manual explained, "the family is the fundamental nucleus of society. . . . Therefore, the material in *analysis is of the greatest importance for the development of the family and national well-being,* and because of this, demands that the employees charged with receiving reports of family violence, specifically the Chilean Police, [give] opportune and efficient attention to those affected" (Carabineros de Chile 1999, p. 22463, emphasis added). In 2005 a new family violence law was instituted (addressed in Chapter 3).

Feminists forced other legal changes to remedy gender inequalities institutionalized in state policies dating back to the Chilean Civil Code of 1857 (see Htun 2003). For example, the Civil Code of 1857 stated that women were to be considered minors under their husbands' care upon marriage. The Relationship Law of 1998 changed this and granted adult women more rights to full citizenship. It also granted all children equal rights before the law, even if born to a single mother. Another major legal change came with the Civil Marriage Law, passed in 2004, which legalized divorce for the first time and made it more equitable for women to separate from husbands. Although these represent real and significant gains in women's rights, Htun (2003) has argued that these legal changes also reflect Chile's goals to *appear* more "developed" and "modern." The picture becomes more complicated when we begin to examine how these novel laws and institutions are reflected in and shape the lives of Marisol, Luz, and Josefina. In-depth ethnographic examination, focused on subjectivities and contexts, complicates "official" pictures.

Entanglements of Violence

Since the publication of the groundbreaking volume on domestic violence by Counts, Brown, and Campbell (1992), a growing body of anthropological literature has illuminated various aspects of women's experiences of gendered violence within local and global contexts (see Wies and Haldane 2011).[17] Recent scholarship has focused on judicial interventions by states and the implications of these interventions within local contexts (Merry 2000). In her transnational, delocalized ethnography Merry shows some of the ways in which United Nations conventions and frameworks are appropriated, rejected, or revised in their translation within local contexts and theorizes that state-level laws and discourses around domestic violence can bring different possibilities for new forms of gendered subjectivity (Merry 2006). As Moore (1994:141, cited in Merry 2006) notes, "individuals constitute their sense of self . . . through several, often mutually contradictory subject positions, rather than through one singular subject position." Merry (2006:186) notes that women "try on" new legal subjectivities and that "gendered subjectivity is redefined by doing legal activities: through acting as a legally entitled subject in the context of these injuries."

Also within a framework of how law and women's experiences of domestic violence interact, Mindie Lazarus-Black (2007) has critiqued the supposed "regendering" of the state in Trinidad, which was to be accomplished in part by the new family violence law there. She shows, through detailed ethnographic research, how problematic time lags in the judicial system's responses to cases of domestic violence, along with the courts' focus on reconciliation, encouraged the majority of women to drop their cases of domestic violence. Similarly, in an ethnography of family courts in India, Srimati Basu (2012) has illuminated how the feminist ideals upon which the mediation process had been based, which were supposed to give women more power and enhance their agency, failed to translate into feminist courtroom practices and failed to bring the gender justice feminist reformers had imagined. She notes that feminist mobilization is rarely if ever "purely incorporated" into state policies. Further, Hautzinger (2007) has shown how women's police stations in Brazil, while providing new forms of protection for women, also have unexpected effects and reproduce gendered power inequalities within the society, a finding that resonates with women's experiences in Chile.

This book adds to scholarship on gender-based violence by focusing intensely on Luz's, Marisol's, and Josefina's subjective, affective experiences as they interact in dialogic relationship over time with the novel state structures—juridical, medical, nongovernmental, and discursive—recently built up around domestic violence; and with women's rights organizations and feminist frameworks. Their intimate narratives tell more than the stories of their individual lives. They show how these women's health, their overall well-being, is affected by various forms of violence that constitute, sustain, and perpetuate what we call domestic violence. And through this analysis it becomes clear that their health is at stake.

Through analysis of the interrelationships and interconstructions of forms of violence and subjectivities, a more nuanced conceptualization of structural violence, a key form of violence that affects health, often in insidious ways, also becomes possible (Biehl and Moran-Thomas 2009). According to Farmer's (2005) elaboration of the framework of structural violence, social inequalities, including poverty, racism, and sexism, are deeply entrenched historical processes that perpetuate suffering and ill health. Structural violence is deeply entangled with domestic violence against women, as anthropologists have shown in a variety of contexts around the globe (Adelman 2004; Alcalde 2010; Wies and Haldane 2011; Merry 2009). Structural violence, in interaction with other forms of violence, provides the conditions of possibility for domestic violence to occur. Structural and domestic violence are also entangled with other forms of violence in local contexts, particularly in Central and South America, where political and state-perpetrated violence were rife in the 1970s and 1980s (see Menjívar 2011).

The Violence of the "Normal"

How do various forms of violence come to be figured as "normal" within specific contexts? Ethnographic knowledge production has shed new light on this question over the past decades. In her seminal work, which expanded our notions of what constitutes violence, Nancy Scheper-Hughes (1992) observed that the structural inequalities that produce starvation in a small, poverty-stricken town in Brazil constitute forms of what she called "everyday violence." Everyday violence is so entrenched in the political and economic structures of everyday life that it becomes invisible and therefore is simply seen as normal. Along similar yet divergent lines, Veena Das has shown through her ethnographic work on the lingering effects of the violence of the partition between India and Pakistan how the extraordinary violence of that critical event and the disruption it caused became folded into ordinary life within families and relationships (Das 2000). Das posits that such violence becomes "poisonous knowledge," shaping the subjective experiences of everyday life in often imperceptible ways, thereby working its way into the "ordinary" and *becoming* the ordinary. Violence, once lived, is always part of oneself and the social fabric. Though violence and its effects can be transformed, violence is never truly over or finished. Instead, traces remain in memories and actions. The transformation of extraordinary violence into ordinary experience, as in the afterlife of the Partition, is different from the notion of everyday violence in Scheper-Hughes's sense, since ordinary violence is the extraordinary violence of a critical event, that, once folded into ordinary life, becomes part of that life, and everyday violence is banal and structurally entrenched. Everyday violence is routine and everyday; it is not an event. Or, by taking Scheper-Hughes's notion of everyday violence in terms of Das's notion of ordinary violence produced from a critical event, we can see that *the everyday is actually an event* that produces poisonous knowledge.

In any case, various forms of violence occur and are perpetuated through processes of normalization. For Bourgois, normalized violence is constituted by the "institutional practices, discourses, cultural values, ideologies, everyday interactions, and routinized bureaucracies that render violence invisible and produce social indifference" (Bourgois 2009:19). That is, through processes of normalization, forms of violence come to be seen as simply "the way things are" (see Jenkins 1996:288).

Also at work in women's experiences of domestic violence is symbolic violence, Bourdieu's concept for the deeply rooted psychological processes through which people internalize their own subjugation as though it were natural and immutable. At the concept's core is the process of "misrecognition," whereby the internalization of discrimination and inequality come to be seen by social actors as "just the way the world is" (Bourdieu and Wacquant 1992). Symbolic violence is highly invisible, as it describes a psychological process of internalization of societal expectations, which are often related to gender and power relationships. Symbolic violence emerges in the narratives of Luz, Marisol, and Josefina and merges with other forms of violence they suffer. Before domestic violence was named as a problem that needed to be addressed, it operated as a form of symbolic violence insofar as it was not seen as a problem. Domestic violence was misrecognized as "normal."

Naming Issues

Men's abuse of women within intimate domestic relationships has been publicly named using various labels (see Merry 2009a). The women's rights movement in the United States originally used the term "domestic violence" to describe this form of social suffering, and the women's rights movement in Chile adopted this name. In SER-NAM's publications, "domestic violence" (*violencia doméstica*) has been the term of choice for naming this violation of women's rights and bodily integrity. In the Chilean judicial system the naming has revolved around conceptualization of the heterosexual, nuclear family, and so in juridical sites the constellation of problems is called "family violence" (*violencia intrafamiliar*). Globally, in the past decade or so, domestic violence has also been subsumed under the label "gender-based violence" or "gender violence," which highlights how social processes of gendering are central to such forms of violence. Another widely used term is "violence against women," which highlights that women as a group are subject to various forms of violence. The phrase "gender-based intimate partner violence against women" can signal a variety of aspects of the problem, including (1) the importance of processes of gender socialization and inequalities, (2) the intimate nature of the violence, and (3) the disproportionate way this form of violence affects women (Parson forthcoming). However, this term still allows the perpetrators of the violence to remain invisible.

Given this wide range of labels, which is best suited to describe women's experiences of the complicated constellations of violence that *Traumatic States* addresses? There is not one. There are many, depending on the context. The political valence and cultural meanings of these different terms are important, and so I have used the various terms where they are most culturally and politically appropriate—in terms of the politics of the various actors within the particular local contexts where I conducted my ethnography. For instance, when talking about the Family Violence Law, I employ the term "family violence"; however, for women who work at Safe Space, the term "family violence" is anathema, so when I address Safe Space, I use the term they used—"domestic violence." At times I also employ various terms in order to speak to other scholars working on issues of domestic, intimate partner, gender-based, and family violence against women. Naming is certainly important; however, it is impossible to encapsulate the real, messy, and complicated contents of the problem in a single category, defined by a fixed label, that is easily applicable to all contexts and situations.

The slipperiness of these terms points to a key tension in naming. Categories are vital in order to provide collective visibility to forms of pain that were formerly invisible—unnamed and unspoken. The terms that have evolved to describe forms of domestic violence have clear political and also moral valence; that is, they describe unacceptable behavior. Naming domestic violence has been crucial to the development of further discursive and material structures that have made it possible for communication about and interventions into this problem. Novel categories for human experience, often technical or juridical, such as "domestic violence," can come to shape experience and even define selves, thereby "making up people" in a process that Hacking calls "dynamic nominalism" (Hacking 1998). Hacking describes how, through the "looping effect," people can come to conceive of themselves through new categories for human experience, thereby in a way becoming those very categories. In the process of dynamic nominalism the tension in naming arises. The people whom the categories describe "come into existence" in the eyes of bureaucratic systems, along with or because of the existence of the categories themselves.

Fassin and Rechtman (2009) posit that such categories can become problematic when they begin to obscure actual suffering and the political and economic interests and arrangements that *produce* social suffering. Their object of study is the diagnostic category PTSD (post-traumatic stress disorder), which, they argue, along with "trauma" more generally, has come to be used around the world as a way of naming and then treating *symptoms*, not underlying etiologies, of psychological distress brought on by political conflicts and other sorts of disasters like earthquakes and tsunamis. They show how the PTSD diagnostic itself has become a major focus of international aid, which demands that people must be "made up" by that category to be seen and to access services. Through the embodiment of PTSD symptoms they can make their suffering legible to the relevant authorities.

When resources are focused on diagnostic categories and psychological phenomena, such as trauma, the focus on the complicated roots of human suffering—often political and economic, or structural—can be neatly ignored. In much the same way, the legalistic naming of domestic violence and psychological and psychiatric therapies built up around it can make reified notions of "domestic violence" the objects of attention, successfully diverting attention from the social forces and inequalities that produce and maintain much human suffering, including domestic violence against women. Through such categorization, people can be "seen" by state and international authorities in a manner that may bring some social change but may not substantially challenge political and economic orders. Focusing on the category of domestic violence instead of the horrifically banal ways that women suffer in their everyday lives makes the issue appear more clear-cut, as though it can be addressed by bureaucracies of the state in predefined and technocratic ways. Within bureaucracies, forms of human experience can come to be seen as unidimensional, easily defined, neat—reified into crystalline categories. It is the categories that are to be seen, not the people. Messy human experiences and complicated social, political, economic, racialized, ethnic, gendered, and cultural realities bracketed outside of these categories can then be deemed superfluous.

By naming the phenomenon "domestic violence" and then intervening with technocratic solutions in judicial and health care systems, the complicated realities that produce that problem can become increasingly hidden behind the label itself. In this way, women who suffer domestic violence can find themselves turned into "bureaucratized selves" subjected, subjugated, and objectified by the very label and systems designed to care for them. Ethnography provides tools to see beyond and through labels in order to illuminate the finer grains of lived human experience.

In different ways, Marisol's, Luz's, and Josefina's subjectivities, along with their pathways to healing and "recovery" and their meanings, are shaped by novel technical and political categories around a new, gendered subject position of "domestic violence victim" and the laws, policies, and practices built around it. "Domestic violence victim" became a new category that served to define a particular gendered subjectivity through which women could experience themselves and their relationships to state and family in new ways. Women who have come to inhabit, appropriate, or reject the new category "domestic violence victim" have seen their suffering, once intimate and unspeakable, transformed into a public object that can be spoken about and that can define them and their rights to make demands on the state (Petryna 2002). Adriana Petryna (2002), in theorizing processes of biological citizenship in the modern state, has identified precisely how the post-Soviet Ukrainian government triaged care based on levels of exposure and related suffering following the Chernobyl nuclear reactor meltdown. Those deemed most afflicted by the radiation fallout, determined by often-arbitrary "scientific" standards, were awarded more of the state's resources, positioning them to claim citizenship based on assessment of their damaged physiology. Similarly, in the catastrophe of intimate partner violence against women in Chile, citizenship is implicitly at stake. However, no matter how severe the intimate partner violence, there is no guarantee of adequate care nor, therefore, a guarantee of full citizenship.

Traumatic States explores the effects this naming has had on how women experience themselves and their worlds. The effects of naming are not top-down; the process of dynamic nominalism is not deterministic. It is a dynamic, dialogic process in which new categories for thinking, naming, and social action interact with individuals' everyday lived experience. And, as women's appropriation, rejection, and reworking make these categories what they are, women themselves find the limits and possibilities of these new discursive frames and the institutional realities that accompany them. That is, forms of gendered subjectivity and agency emerge not only in response to new juridical and technical categories, but they also spring independently from a human drive for meaning.

As Cristina Alcalde has so poignantly shown in her ethnography of women who live in the marginal intersections of poverty, racism, and domestic violence on the outskirts of Lima, Peru, even within a situation of severe suffering, women assert their agency, however constrained agency may be and always is (Alcalde 2010; see also Parson 2010a). Indeed, as Das (2000:210) has noted, "Individual lives are defined by context, but they are also generative of new contexts." Deep, experience near ethnographic engagement allowed for exploration of Luz, Marisol, and Josefina's desires for and their capacity to generate new contexts, along with their needs for material, intellectual, emotional, and legal resources to do so. Through ethnographic engagement in the lives of Luz, Marisol, and Josefina, I explore their desires for and capacity to generate new contexts, as well as the material, intellectual, emotional, and legal resources they need to do so. What allows Marisol, Josefina, and Luz to engage in processes of generating new contexts and reworking violence and suffering? What prevents them from such a reworking and impedes their processes of healing? Ethnographic, close attention to the nuances of the ethos, constituted by the ethical and moral contours of historical, political, economic, and societal contexts, is fundamental to answering these questions (see Kleinman 1999).

Neoliberal Regimes and Ethics of Care

Traumatic States contends that in postdictatorship Chile the moral contours of care seeking for domestic violence were shaped by forms of feminism and neoliberal individualism, two opposing frameworks for understanding social relationships, power relationships, and the fundamental goals of human life. Local context matters in thinking about what feminist and neoliberal individualism mean and are. There is no one feminism—there are many (see Mohanty 1991), and this has been widely asserted through critiques of the racism, heterosexism, ethnocentrism, classism, colonialism, and other forms of bias inherent in "Western" forms of feminism (see Abu-Lughod 2002). Similarly, neoliberal individualism manifests differently in diverse local contexts. As Tsing (2005) has argued, it is crucial to examine how neoliberal regimes interact in specific local contexts, "where the rubber hits the road" and "friction" is produced.

Neoliberal political and economic systems are also moral and ethical systems. The values of neoliberalism seep into all sorts of moral holes, shaping people's senses of themselves and their ideas about their relationships with others (see Held 2006). Policies based in neoliberal ideologies and economic interests structure care and imply decisions about whose life has value and whose life does not. Agamben (1995) refers to human life deemed to be valueless as "bare life" without citizenship rights, and posits that all societies have mechanisms for either implicitly or explicitly deciding whose life has value and whose is disposable. Medical anthropologists Rylko-Bauer and Farmer (2002), for example, have identified how decisions about the disposability of the lives of people who live in poverty happens in the United States through market-based health care, or "managed care." Rylko-Bauer and Farmer argue that the creation and dependence on managed care systems in the United States have undermined health care for society's most vulnerable, leading to "managed inequality," that is, care for some and not for others. In a system of managed inequality, those with resources receive care and those without do not, or they receive inadequate care. This, at its base, is the neoliberal ethic—that those who have the most resources are those who "deserve" care the most.[18]

Feminism, as manifest in the Chilean women's movement, which has structured both state and nongovernmental care for women who suffer domestic violence since the late 1980s, is based on a critique of the gender inequalities between men and women that structure society, though not in a deterministic fashion, and influence all sorts of relationships in various ways. The feminist movement in Chile has sought to shift unequal power relationships between men and women in various spheres of life, and as part of this have struggled to provide women who suffer domestic violence with care that addresses these inequalities. In contrast to a society based in the neoliberal paradigm of individual responsibility and shrinking state responsibility, a society based on a feminist ethic of care, Held posits, "requires us to pay attention to, rather than ignore, the material, psychological, and social pre-requisites for autonomy" (Held 2006:84).[19] A feminist ethic of care entails "thinking of persons as relational, and conceptualizing society and its institutions in the light of the values of care and caring activities" (76). In much the same way as feminism argues that the personal is political, an ethic of care promotes care beyond the family and other intimate ties to political spheres. An ethic of care largely conflicts with neoliberal values of individualism, self-efficacy, and self-responsibility. Based on an analysis of women's narratives and ethnographic examination of some of their life contexts, *Traumatic States* explores how the state's forms of care in Chile are largely based on a neoliberal ethic of individual responsibility and market logics, whereas a feminist ethic of care, exhibited by Safe Space and many women's rights proponents and political reformers in Chile, provides a basis for long-term engagement with women's suffering produced from intimate, gendered violence.

Methodological Notes: Ethnographic Engagements[20]

Through ethnographic engagement within some of the local ecologies of care (Das and Das 2007) for women who suffered domestic violence in Santiago, I was able to contextualize the life history narratives of Luz, Marisol, Josefina, and other women as they constructed them in conversation with me. Safe Space, a nongovernmental women's rights organization, and Family Care, originally funded by the Chilean government and then by the municipality where it resided, were key sites for my ethnographic work between 2002 and 2004. Both of these agencies grew out of the Chilean feminist movement's attention to domestic violence. This shared origin point made Safe Space and Family Care ideal sites for ethnographic examination of some of the institutional contexts of women's care-seeking for domestic violence: both sites were originally based on feminist paradigms but evolved in different ways largely because of political and economic contingencies and pressures.

Safe Space and Family Care represent linking points between women's experiences of help-seeking for domestic violence and global feminist frameworks and movements. These agencies are also points in the circuitous movements and "translations" that take place among local, national, and global frameworks and practices that address gender violence. Translations in this sense constitute multidirectional and multidimensional processes. *Traumatic States* examines such translations as they have occurred within local contexts in Chile, with a variety of social actors doing the translations, including women's rights proponents, activists, and organizations; governmental institutions, policies, laws, and officials; agencies like Safe Space and Family Care; and women who have suffered domestic violence themselves.

Safe Space

Safe Space, where I first visited in 2000, was founded in the mid-1980s as a nongovernmental, nonprofit organization to address issues related to women's rights. After the official transition to democracy began in 1990, Safe Space engaged in activism to promote women's rights in a variety of spheres, while avoiding co-optation as a "subcontractor" of SERNAM.[21] During the 1990s they promoted women's full citizenship and participation during the transitional period from dictatorship to official democracy. To this end, they conducted outreach programs, including workshops and community education programs, to educate women in a variety of realms about their rights as citizens and how to exercise these rights. Their work on domestic violence was one aspect of this wider project, and in the early 1990s they began offering integrated services for women in their municipality who had suffered domestic violence. Since then Safe Space has been a leader in addressing women's experiences of domestic violence from a gender inequality perspective and promoting women's active citizenship and participation in civil society as fundamental to preventing and addressing the suffering caused by domestic violence. However, by 2002 Safe Space had ceased offering aid to women who had suffered domestic violence because the new mayor had by then retracted their funding.

I met Ema at Safe Space in 2001 during my second visit there, in her office where publications and posters about women's rights and domestic violence lined the cheery yellow walls. Ema has been one of the most enduring members of Safe Space, part of the organization almost since its inception in the 1980s. Ema and I quickly became good friends and shared countless conversations over meals and coffee or on our way to or from Safe Space's office. Ema introduced me to Safe Space's work, other staff members, and the wider contexts of Chilean politics and women's rights issues and activism, especially in Safe Space's municipality. She also told me about how her activism and political awareness came from her mother, who had been a proponent of social justice during Allende's presidency and was later tortured by Pinochet's dictatorial regime. The Chilean state had waged its violence on her mother's body and mind when they arrested and then savagely tortured her because she was involved in the movement for class equality under Allende. Ema was only fourteen years old at the time, and she, the eldest sibling, was left to take care of the family. Ema continued her mother's activism for social justice, engaging in antidictatorship activism and later feminist activism, out of which Safe Space had originally grown. Many of the other women who worked at Safe Space had also protested the dictatorial repression and rampant class inequalities endemic in Chilean society.

My ethnographic engagements with Safe Space in 2002 through 2004 included attending their public events, rallies, marches to protest violence against women, seminars, and workshops. I also met with and interviewed various staff members. Ema facilitated my contact with ten women who had suffered domestic violence and sought help there, and they shared their life history narratives with me. The patterns of interaction and interviewing differed depending on each woman's availability and particular desire for how the research process would progress. I developed friendships and deeper relationships with some, while with others the relationships remained more structured within the terms of researcher and interviewee, although I attempted to minimize such barriers and to highlight the research process as a collaborative endeavor between the women and me. I interviewed the women with whom I forged friendships, and, as time went on, other conversations and experiences outside of the designated interview sessions informed my understanding of their situations and their healing processes. I built this type of collaborative relationship most notably with Marisol and Luz, who also chose to increase their involvement in my project over time. The production of anthropological, ethnographic knowledge is, in essence, a collaborative project.

Marisol and Luz both invited me to participate with them in various events related to women's rights activism, which gave me a more well-rounded understanding of the importance of these activities in their lives. Through Luz I became briefly involved with some of the activities of a grassroots women's organization called the Women's Place, which had close ties to Safe Space, and where Luz had been quite active. We also had meals together and discussed topics beyond their experiences of domestic violence. As women a generation older, they acted as mentors and as guides for me within the Chilean context, informed as it is by particular historical events and cultural patterns. I gathered their life histories through ongoing and numerous interviews, in addition to unrecorded conversations. With the other women I interviewed at Safe Space, I developed fruitful relationships but not ongoing friendships.

My research relationships, especially with Marisol and Luz but with other women I interviewed as well, were marked by intersubjective engagement; the ethnographic processes in which we mutually engaged affected us both. Scheper-Hughes (1992:25) has cogently noted that in this deeply intersubjective exchange, both researcher and participant have particular stakes. As she says, "Anthropological knowledge may be seen as something produced in human interaction, not merely 'extracted' from naïve informants who are unaware of the hidden agendas coming from the outsider" (25).

Family Care

In the early 1990s, Family Care was founded as one of the first state-funded centers to work with women who had suffered domestic violence. The founders of Family Care were feminist women's rights activists, linked to feminists who were founding members of SERNAM. Their work was originally based on the feminist axiom that domestic violence against women has its roots in gendered inequalities within a patriarchal society. At its inception Family Care served women who had experienced domestic violence as well as children who were victims of abuse. Later, Family Care incorporated a treatment program for male abusers. The entire staff at Family Care, which consisted of four teams focused on prevention, male abusers, children who lived in abusive situations, and women who suffered domestic violence, usually met once a week. I attended those weekly meetings for ten months, in addition to the weekly meetings of the team focused specifically on women who had suffered domestic violence. These meetings generally lasted for two or three hours, with at least a half hour devoted to breakfast and socializing. This structure allowed me to become familiar with the center's daily workings, to learn about the most pressing issues they faced, and to form relationships with key staff members. I conducted structured, semistructured, and unstructured interviews with several of the staff members.

Each week I also attended the staff meeting of the team working with women. These meetings usually lasted around two hours and were attended by two or three therapists, the lawyer, the social worker, and occasionally the center's director. Discussions at these meetings focused on coordinating cases. Staff members also talked about more general issues, such as time constraints, diagnostics, and program objectives. At these meetings, I generally took notes, practiced active listening, asked questions, and offered input where appropriate. These meetings allowed me to build relationships with these key staff members; to learn the ways they discussed their work, their clients, and their perspectives; and to identify important underlying themes and problems in their work with women and how the larger social context influenced them.

I also observed group therapy sessions for one six-month interval in order to learn more about the therapeutic context and women's lives and healing experiences. The group met once a week for two hours. The women's team found this to be an excellent idea and encouraged me to take on a role in the group as cofacilitator, as they said it was ideal to have two people leading the sessions. I agreed to this although I explained that I did not want to take too pronounced a role because I am not trained as a therapist. Another motivation for avoiding too dominant a role was that my main goal was to learn about the group therapy there and women's responses to it. I did not seek to investigate how my presence would change this (although of course it did), nor to investigate how my ideas were being received. For these reasons, I chose to offer small bits of my own insight or perspective but tried to do so judiciously.

In order to facilitate some informal space for women to gather and talk after each group session, I offered to provide coffee, tea, and snacks and to keep the room open following the therapy sessions. During the final session, the women took it upon themselves to organize a Chilean Independence Day party, complete with dancing the national dance, *la cueca*, and serving homemade empanadas. Each week I arrived early to set up the room with the chairs in a circle, to prepare the "teatime" fare, and to talk informally with women who arrived prior to the official start of the group. Many women stayed afterward to talk informally and expressed thanks for this space and time to gather in a more relaxed and unstructured format. This "teatime" also gave me the opportunity to get to know some of the women in a different way and facilitated the process of engaging them in fruitful life history interviews (with the approval of the therapist). All but one of the eight women who had suffered domestic violence whom I interviewed through Family Care had participated in this group. As a result of my experiences with the group therapy sessions, I decided to also invite the women to partici-pate in group interviews. I conducted a monthlong series of four group interviews, each lasting two to three hours. During these interviews I focused on gathering information about their perspectives on their experiences of domestic violence as informed by the wider societal context. Seven women participated in the group interviews (although each did not necessarily participate in all four sessions). Four of these women also participated in individual interviews, and four additional women participated only in individual interviews but not the group ses-sions. Therefore, through Family Care I interviewed a total of eleven women about their experiences of domestic violence and recovery. I met Josefina at Family Care, and she was eager to share the story of her lifetime of extreme suffering with me. I interviewed and talked infor-mally with her at Family Care many times in 2003 and again when I visited in 2009.

Women's Experiential Knowledge

Detachment is neither a natural gift nor a manufactured
talent. It is a partial achievement laboriously earned and
precariously maintained. —Clifford Geertz (2000:39)

Every view is a view from somewhere and every act of speaking,
a speaking from somewhere. —Lila Abu-Lughod (1991:141)

Women's life history narratives give more visibility to contexts of suffering and care for women who suffered domestic violence as it began to
be recognized by various state and nonstate actors. Although eighteen
women shared their life history narratives with me, the narratives of
Josefina, Marisol, and Luz are the focus of *Traumatic States* because
of the long-term nature of our engagements. I interviewed and talked
informally with them over the course of six years, from 2003 to 2009.
Life history narrative analysis can produce a crucial form of knowledge
through a focus on how the self is "embedded in historical context but
not reducible to it" as Maynes, Pierce, and Laslett (2008:67) have put
it.[22] The deeply interior experiential knowledge that Marisol, Josefina,
and Luz shared with me provides the basis upon which I, as an anthropologist, can produce scholarly knowledge about how their subjective
senses of themselves are in part shaped, though not completely determined, by their relationships to key societal structures, including the
judicial system and organizations like Family Care and Safe Space.
Many other women I interviewed voiced similar experiences and concerns to those of Marisol, Luz, and Josefina. So, these three women's
narratives are their own, *and* they are reflections of other women's
narratives in many ways. Although their lives are heavily marked by
extraordinary suffering, in many ways this extraordinary suffering is actually quite ordinary, a form of the "routinized misery" (Kleinman and
Kleinman 1997) of gender-based intimate partner violence that has
shaped so many women's subjectivities and possibilities in life across
cultures. Life history narrative analysis is a form of social science that
goes against a tendency whereby "much of routinized misery is in-

visible; much that is made visible is not ordinary or routine" (Kleinman et al. 1997a:xiii).

In order to ethically conduct this research and representation, I forged emotionally engaged affective connections with the women who appear in this ethnography, especially Marisol and Luz. The real challenge in the ethical practice of research on subjectivity is the emotional negotiation involved. That is, as a researcher I thought constantly about how to be both an *emotionally engaged, vulnerable* observer, as Ruth Behar (1996; see also Sanford and Angel-Ajani 2006) suggests, and a *detached* observer. As Geertz puts it, there are many "difficulties of being at one and the same time an involved actor and a detached observer" (Geertz 2000:39). Grappling with this gray area is crucial for the production of ethnographic knowledge about intimate forms of violence and subjectivities.

Informed by a generation of feminist anthropology (Lamphere, Ragoné, and Zavella 1997; Moore 1988, 1994; Ortner 1996) and by feminist work on women's rights as human rights (Bunch and Carrillo 1991; Carrillo, Bunch, and Shore 1998; Turshen 2007), I felt it was my ethical imperative to offer information, consolation, and encouragement where I deemed it appropriate during the course of my interviews and sometimes friendships with my interlocutors. Of course, this likely altered their narratives, in imperceptible ways, but it also allowed them to continue and allowed for the production of knowledge based on their expressions of their own experiences. I could not stand idly by in a stance of "objective" observation to watch a person suffer through the telling of a painful story without offering some words of empathy and compassion and at times ideas for reworking the painful memories in new ways. As Marisol pointed out to me in reference to her experiences with incompetent judicial officials: sometimes listening is not enough.[23] I attempted to maintain a stance of both vulnerable and detached observation. Such reflexivity, to a certain extent, is fundamental to the practice of ethnographic research (Behar and Gordon 1995; Clifford, Marcus, and School of American Research 1986; Gordon 1988; Personal Narratives Group 1989).

Because issues of domestic violence are very delicate, investigations of the lived realities of domestic violence must happen within environments marked by safety for the women who have suffered. It can be dangerous for women to come forward to seek help or to participate in an interview. In light of these potential risks, my ethnographic engagement with Safe Space and Family Care allowed for the ethical conduct of this research. I knew that the women I talked with had at the least some access to services and had sought out that access themselves.

An Engaged Imagination and Representations of Violence

How is it that so many women across the globe suffer violence against them by intimates and yet this form of suffering continues to be largely invisible? How does desensitization to violence and suffering in our midst play a role in this pandemic? Kleinman and Kleinman's (1997) analysis of a Pulitzer Prize–winning photograph of a dying Sudanese girl, ribs almost tearing through her paper-thin skin, with a vulture at her side awaiting her death, is instructive here. They note that, in order to document this tragedy, the photographer waited for quite some time, snapping many frames before arriving at the prize-winning image that eventually circulated the globe. Meanwhile, the emaciated child, who remained nameless and without social context, died. Ultimately, Kleinman and Kleinman point here to one of *the* greatest ethical issues of our times—that we can witness others' suffering at a distance, meanwhile feeling unable, or actually being unable, to act upon that suffering (see also Agamben 1999).

This book constitutes an act of bearing witness and asserts that this act implies a responsibility on the part of the witness to in some way address the "poisonous knowledge" (Das 2000) of violence. The traces of this representation of violence and suffering may linger in the reader's "engaged imagination," which Kirmayer (2007:378) argues is "the only faculty we have that lets us see beyond the horizon of convention." With the imagination engaged, readers can enter the life worlds of the women who are the protagonists of *Traumatic States*. As many of the contexts and intimate subjective states of Josefina, Luz, and Marisol will be previously unknown to many readers, I endeavor to make it possible to enter into these lives and some of their contingencies and complications. The reader's imagination provides a bridge to make that possible and is crucial in the attempt to circumvent what Elaine Scarry (1985) has identified as pain's resistance to language, the inexpressibility of pain.[24] As pain destroys language, the women's narratives that constitute the foundation of *Traumatic States* are testaments to the possibilities, and difficulties, of recuperating language and are attempts to express the inexpressible *and* to be heard. Witnesses are necessary for hearing to occur, and not just anyone can adequately and with care and sensitivity serve as a witness. Care requires training and skill for particular kinds of situations. Care that is particularly designed for women who have suffered domestic violence has been in development for only around four decades worldwide, and for only two decades in Chile. Family Care and Safe Space both offered a version of this kind of care for women who suffered domestic violence in Santiago, and both no longer offer such care. The provision of skilled caregiving by those with vast experience in helping women out of the hole of domestic violence is precarious. It is contingent on political will and funding. It is contingent on political ideologies and on women's willingness to seek the care that is offered.

Chapter Outline

Taken as a whole, *Traumatic States* reveals how Luz, Marisol, and Josefina suffer various entanglements of violence that call for diverse and interdisciplinary forms of care.[25] It argues that the state's novel forms of care, created in relationship with nongovernmental organizations like Safe Space, are in many ways helpful for women's reworking of the poisonous knowledge of violence. However, at the same time, the state's forms of care neglect the complicated entanglements and interconstructions of the forms of violence that women like Josefina, Luz, and Marisol embody. *Traumatic States* shows how the failure to adequately identify and intervene in these violent entanglements leads state structures of care to cause further suffering, often becoming *part of* the suffering of domestic violence. *Traumatic States* shows how the state's biopolitical structures ostensibly aimed at care are at times forms of social control instead of care.

Chapters 2 and 3 constitute an analysis of Marisol's life history narratives, multiple informal meetings I had with her, and court-related documents she shared with me that detail her entrance into the bureaucracy of the state via the judicial system, from 1996 to 2009. Chapter 2 focuses on her experiences in the judicial system under the first Family Violence Law of 1994 and her health problems and interactions with psychological and medical care providers. Chapter 3 continues to trace Marisol's trajectory through care-seeking in judicial and medical systems, this time under the reformed Family Violence Law of 2005. Marisol's experiences illuminate how bureaucracy can function to allow for impunity and distancing—the normalization of violence through the state's novel juridical and medical interventions. Chapter 4 focuses on Josefina to illuminate the entanglements of state, symbolic, normalized, structural, and intimate forms of gendered violence in her experience. Josefina's family was affected by the dictatorial state's persecution, and this chapter highlights how the state's violence and repression interacted with domestic violence to produce ongoing suffering for her. Her narratives highlight how, although the causes of her suffering were social in nature, the remedies offered to her were often psychiatric and psychotherapeutic—aimed firmly at Josefina's interior emotional state. Based centrally on an analysis of Luz's narratives from 2003 and 2009, Chapter 5 highlights tensions between the "creativity of everyday life"[26] and constrained agency. It raises the critical question: How do imagination and creativity engender survival under duress, under the violent regimes of dictatorship, domestic violence, and neoliberal policies, to mention a few of the instances of structural inequality poor and lower-middle-class women in Chile often face? The arc of Luz's narrative also highlights how the knowledge of violence, while it can be transformed, still moves her life.

Together, the first five chapters show how continuous care of various sorts for Marisol, Luz, and Josefina is crucial because of the iterative nature of their processes of healing. Chapter 6 examines how, in spite of this established need for continuous care for women who suffer domestic violence, care is often contingent on political and economic contexts and power dynamics instead of being grounded in an ongoing ethic of care. Chapter 6 draws from my ethnographic engagements with SERNAM, Safe Space, and Family Care to show how contexts of care for Luz, Marisol, and Josefina are constantly shifting and how new structures present new challenges for adequate and continuous care. Chapter 7 concludes with an argument for understanding and addressing the health and health care needs of women who have suffered domestic violence in terms of the particular intimate, local, national, and global forces involved in producing and providing continuous care for women who undergo this form of suffering. It illuminates how inequalities produce the damage suffered by women like Luz, Marisol, and Josefina. Therefore, the inequalities, not the individuals who incur the damage, constitute the locus of pathology and cure. The emotional trauma that Luz, Marisol, and Josefina have experienced can never be fully assessed or addressed, and violence, once lived, produces situations that can only be worked through, not erased. The state's resources that Marisol, Luz, and Josefina have claimed have ultimately fallen short of enabling them the possibilities to engage in meaningful healing.

CHAPTER 2

Feeling the State's Gaze
on Intimate Violence

One Friday evening in March 2003, as dusk settled over Santiago, I watched Ema pore over Safe Space's files, filled with cases of women who had suffered violence by men with whom they had lived and shared a life. I remember each of the women Ema introduced me to over the phone that evening, but Marisol chose to build a friendship with me in a way that none of the other women I spoke with that night did. From that moment onward, we actively sought each other out and allowed our lives to intertwine with the common goal of documenting her experiential knowledge of violence and processes of healing, through the narrative coproduction of her life story—with her as narrator of her pain and me as listener. Marisol has engaged with this study as part of her life's project of reworking meaning for herself and reworking gendered meanings and inequalities in society. "I always say that what I fought for will serve as an example for my daughters, or for other women and their daughters," she told me. "That's what I've done, fighting for women's rights, for their children, for dignity, for justice. I think that's my leitmotif. There's no other. I am going to fight and fight and continue fighting."

As of 2010, I had known Marisol and followed her life for more than seven years. I met with her many times when she still lived in her home in Santiago, which was legally the property of her husband, Gerardo. The house was a two-story home with three bedrooms—a nice space, where Marisol knew her neighbors and was the block leader. Marisol and I have had countless conversations over the years we have known one another: at her house, as she sped me to the subway in her van after a brief court encounter related to a public hearing (discussed in Chapter 6), and in my home. After completing my long-term fieldwork during 2002 and 2003, I returned to the United States, and Marisol and I maintained contact through sporadic phone calls and via e-mail. We exchanged news and pictures, which pieced us together until my next visits to Chile in 2006, 2009, and 2011. Since I have known Marisol and interviewed her sporadically over the course of eight years, I have a long-term perspective on the ways that the actions and inactions of the state have shaped her life and her mindful body (see Scheper-Hughes and Lock 1987).

Marisol's Life History Narrative

Marisol felt lucky that she had grown up surrounded by a close-knit family, in a moderately sized port town on the Chilean coast. She was raised in her grandmother's house. "We lived in a democracy [in our house]," she told me. Her family's strong beliefs in the importance of education and in the formation of a social conscience were the guiding principles of her childhood, parts of which she remembered quite fondly, though other parts, she told me in our later visits, were quite painful. Her father worked in a large textile factory, but his true passion was art, which Marisol reflected on happily. She talked lovingly about his influence on her life. She learned to explore her creativity with her father, painting and making pottery with him. He fused his interest in art with his social consciousness to perform public health–oriented puppet shows and to host meetings about fine arts.

Marisol told me proudly of how her mother and grandmother constantly helped others through their work with the church, tending to the sick and those affected by death. They fulfilled dominant gender-role expectations for women to perform caring labor that maintained community and family cohesion. In addition, "They all taught me to take care of my husband, give him respect. They only taught what they were taught," Marisol said, commenting on the strongly rooted nature of *machista* (sexist, patriarchal) values in Chilean society, passed down through the generations.

Both of Marisol's parents achieved a sixth-grade education and greatly valued education for their eight children. By age seven, Marisol was focused on her goal of attending university. In 1963, at age eleven, she moved to Santiago to study in a teacher's college for four years. After she finished her high school education she was forced to return home for health reasons. She soon entered university in a nearby town where she studied for five years to be a teacher. She continued to develop a strong social conscience there. She participated in Mapuche cultural activities, the university chorus, and community service. After university, once back home, Marisol constructed workshops to help teachers use art as a tool for learning. She talked proudly of the positive outcomes of these workshops and her ability to help students reach their potential. For Marisol, teaching was a part of her life's project that was truncated by Gerardo's abuse and control and that she later brought to her work with other women who were abused.

Marisol was in her late twenties when she married Gerardo. He was in his early forties, with a prior marriage and two daughters. "Even after fifteen days of marriage," she lamented, "I realized that it was a mistake, that I really didn't know him. I didn't know what he thought. I didn't talk to him. What I thought I knew, I didn't really know." Marisol continued:

My mother felt that from her perspective it was a good idea, and everything was okay. But for me it was really traumatic. . . . Really, I think she didn't realize how he really was, because he has two personalities, one personality for his partner and the other for everyone else. It was very hard to satisfy him. Nothing ever made him happy or satisfied.

Every day he got up, ate breakfast which I fixed for him, left the house and then returned at night and expected that I serve him food. He ate and read the newspaper, and then we went to bed. And that was my life as a married woman. And I asked myself, "What am I going to do with all of my free time?" He didn't want me to work [outside the home]. . . . I was extremely in love with him, and so I told him that I wanted to talk to him [about this]. He said, "Okay, once you're done with your womanly duties and chores, then we can talk." So I told him that if this was to be our married life everyday, there was a problem. He said, "No. I only discuss when there's a real problem."

"When I realized that I had made this huge mistake," she continued, "I was overcome by a very difficult depression. . . . After the first three months [of marriage] I went to a psychiatrist."

Marisol explained her view of how violence affected the life of her mind:

> the violence affects one's health because one is affected
> psychologically when she realizes that she can't develop herself as
> a person. . . . You have to start to lie. They oblige you to lie. . . . To
> survive, you have to lie . . . in daily life. . . . [One always has to be
> thinking,] "How am I going to make this situation look like *he wants it
> to be?*" Not how it *is*, or how it happened, or how it would be right. . . .
> She spends a lot of time thinking about how she can give him what he
> wants, how to make him happy.

For nearly the first twenty years of their marriage, Marisol endured the abuse and control practically in silence. Then, in 1996 Marisol first broke her silence about the domestic violence she suffered by talking to a government official in her local municipality office. Prior to that, the state was still very much involved in her intimate life insofar as it maintained an almost palpable absence, but in 1996 she knew the Family Violence Law was in effect and had decided put it to use.

"For many years I had been waiting for the law," she told me, proudly. "I always told my husband when he was violent with me, 'There will be a day when a law will exist in Chile, and I will be the first to go and use it.' . . . And he laughed and said, 'Right! Just for *you* they're going to make a law.'"

While she narrated the initial instantiation of her private suffering in the public sphere, Marisol leaned toward me, as if to emphasize the importance of what she was about to share. She told me: "This was *very* important for me. He [the municipality official whom she first told about the abuse] told me, 'Señora Marisol, no se preocupe porque está todo el estado trabajando para usted' [Señora Marisol, don't worry, because the whole state is working for you]."

In addition to offering her what she felt was very appropriate emotional support, this municipality official referred her to the women's organization nearby, which she had often passed by, wanting to go inside. She explained that she had never had the strength (ánimo) to knock on the door and tell her story until she was "sent" there in 1996 by the municipality official. "I was lucky because I arrived at the right place," Marisol told me, "They attended to me very well. There, I started to have the first support from the state."

In spite of this state intervention Gerardo continued with the abuse so Marisol decided that it was time to file a complaint against him. Marisol was certain to tell her daughters what this would mean for her and for them. She explained:

> It meant we were going to separate, that we were going to live a different kind of life, that we were going to be poor again, that we were going to live alone, that we were going to have to be self-sufficient, and that we were going to have to fight against the entire society. . . . I understood clearly that if one separated, one separated from the family, friendships, and networks one had.

Marisol's expectations for what would happen both to her and to her daughters when they filed this complaint were shaped by her sense that social ruptures of all sorts, in every sphere of society—"the entire society"—were going to occur.[1]

After filing the complaints against Gerardo:

> Things happened as I had said they would. We got poorer. We lost our networks, family, friendships, but we kept going. We kept going in the sense that I kept working. I didn't allow myself to stay in bed even one day with depression or anything. Every day I said to myself: You can't stay here. You have to work. You have to help your daughters get ahead. . . . The truth is that my self-esteem was destroyed, with all of the insults [from her husband], *that I was useless, that I wasn't good for anything, that I was a burden to society, that I had to kill myself because I wasn't useful for society, that I would do society a favor by killing myself, that the only solution to his problems, for him, was to kill myself.* (emphasis added)

"To this I said, 'No. I will not permit it,'" she told me, defying her tears by continuing to talk. These ruptures became an important part of her shared life with her daughters.

"[Sometimes I think] I am responsible," she said, "because if I had ended it [the relationship] in time. . . . OK, I tried to do it. It's true."

"Exactly," I said, "You tried."

"I tried. It didn't work," she replied. "With one daughter I felt like I had the strength to liberate myself from him," she said, and continued: "But with two daughters, I felt too obligated, not in terms of emotions, but in the sense of not taking away my daughters' rights to have a father. Because I still thought that it was good for children to have both mother and father."

Through knowing laughter, she exclaimed, "I wasn't so evolved!" Marisol's experiences of suffering, seeking help, interventions, and recovery, as she has narrated them, have been wound up with her relationship with her daughters. Her subjectivity is shaped by her involvement with them, their lives, and her concern over *their* subjective experiences. She told me, even though I had not asked, "My daughters lived the whole process with me, everything, the whole process from start to finish." At her own mention that the process was "finished," she smiled, looked confidently and proudly at me, and said, "I mean the end we still don't know, but I think we're almost there (*en línea derecha*)."

Marisol's face clouded over when she talked about what happened when her case finally went to court. She felt that the court clerk mistreated her by favoring Gerardo and failing to take her testimony seriously. She expressed that Gerardo was able to "win her [the judge] over to his side," by making himself seem *simpático* (nice, friendly). Marisol speculated: "She didn't handle it well because either she didn't have the tools, or simply, it was so new for her, to know how to enter into the private lives of other people. She was motivated more to listen than *hacer justicia* [do justice]."

Marisol never talked to a lawyer or a judge. She and Gerardo were both ordered to engage in psychological therapy, with the goal of reconciling their differences and continuing as a couple. Marisol, as other

women I interviewed, was critical of the court's focus on reconciliation, written into the 1994 Family Violence Law. Her description of
her problematic experience of this system resonated with what a lawyer
at Family Care revealed to me:

> [Judges and court clerks] insist a lot on trying to finalize the case
> with a reconciliation agreement. That is where women complain
> and say, "I felt forced to sign." . . . This is one of women's permanent
> critiques . . . that they felt obliged to sign the agreements even
> though they were not very clear on what that meant. Because of
> that we accompany them [in the process]. When we are there, the
> pressure for her to agree is less because we are there. So the clerk
> does not dare to pressure the woman because she is with someone
> who is representing her. . . . That is when a real possibility exists for
> discussing important issues and for producing agreements that are
> beneficial for the client.

If no agreement was reached in the first instance, the process could
continue until one was reached, if the accuser so desired.

The process of reconciliation was the foundational principle for
women's encounters with the judicial system until the reform of the
Family Violence Law in 2005. In the region and globally, the focus
on reconciliation in domestic violence cases has become common
(Kwiatkowski 2011; Lazarus-Black 2007). In the narratives of women
I interviewed it became clear that the judicial emphasis on reconciliation served to individualize women's experiences of domestic violence
by conceptualizing such violence as occurring in the decontextual-
ized space of the malfunctioning intimate relationship, which both
individuals (the perpetrator and the victim) were equally responsible
for fixing (see also El Agua Consultores Asociados 1997). This thereby
depoliticized women's experiences of domestic violence and their attempts at help-seeking through state systems. In these and other ways,
reconciliation geared toward repairing and maintaining relationships
damaged by violence can serve to silence suffering and gender inequi-
ties for women seeking justice for domestic violence.

Lazarus-Black (2007) has attributed a similar drive toward reconciliation in domestic violence court cases in Trinidad to a "culture of reconciliation," wherein most cases are terminated with an "undertaking." In an undertaking, perpetrators of domestic violence admit to the violence and agree not to abuse again. Women are encouraged to reconcile with their abusers, or at least to give them a "second chance." For Lazarus-Black this reflects a culture of reconciliation, which she identifies as a major factor in the maintenance of power and gender inequality in the justice system in Trinidad.[2] The culture of reconciliation works to put the onus for justice outside of the justice system by filtering out most cases of domestic violence.

It is important to note that reconciliation in domestic violence cases in the particular context of Chile also reflected a national context in which the Truth and Reconciliation Commission had just released its report exposing many of the human rights violations of the dictatorship era and in which state and society were negotiating reconciliation at the national level following those atrocities. Efforts were made by the Truth and Reconciliation Commission to keep the "national family" together, just as reconciliation was a cornerstone of the 1994 Family Violence Law.[3]

The Good Citizen

For Marisol to receive legal attention, a psychological evaluation was ordered by the court, an instantiation of the juridical-medical complex that women must go through to receive certain kinds of state aid for the problem of domestic violence. For Marisol's suffering of domestic violence to be fully taken into account and "read" by the state, professional validation and naming of her suffering were necessary.

Marisol, a "good citizen" (Biehl 2007) and a "good victim" (Merry 2006), sought the court-mandated psychotherapy and psychological evaluation at her municipality's mental health center (*centro de salud mental*). In a report from the mental health center in September 1997, which Marisol shared with me in 2009, the psychiatrist noted a diagnosis of major depression (*depresión mayor*). The report states:

[Marisol has been] treated since February 1997 with irregular
response to treatment, due to her presentation of a long history of
family violence, characterized by verbal and physical abuse on the
part of her husband, who is 61 years old. This situation has led her
to present multiple symptoms, characterized by pain in the inferior
abdominal region and lumbar, investigated in multiple exams
that show no alterations attributable to a specific organic illness
(*enfermedad orgánica específica*), rather more associated with her
emotional problem. . . . She refers to having had psychiatric treatment
for this problem and a supposed Organ Neurosis (*Neurosis Orgánica*)
without current treatment. Her husband is described as a violent
person, denigrating and aggressive, who was evaluated and treated by
a specialist for only one month, and the patient decided to abandon
[treatment] because of economic problems.

Organ neurosis is a psychoanalytic categorization first developed
by Freud that covers a range of medically unexplained physical symptoms; since its 1980 edition the American Psychiatric Association's
Diagnostic and Statistical Manual no longer includes neuroses. The
range of symptoms characterizing organ neurosis is sometimes referred
to as "medically unexplained physical symptoms." This process of naming Marisol's "disorder" in terms of psychological diagnostic terminolo-
gies is reminiscent of Charcot's diagnosis of "hysterical neuroses" and
Freud's theories of hysteria for women in distress (Pietikäinen 2007;
Young 1995).

The psychiatric diagnosis of major depression was a great support
for Marisol's situation because it provided "proof" that she was a "victim." This assessment proved that she was suffering psychologically in a
way commonly seen in victims of domestic violence. She herself could
provide "testimony," a form of subjective knowledge. However, professionals in the juridical-medical complex had to provide the "truth," the
real, technical knowledge about her situation (see Foucault and Gordon 1980) for it to be considered legitimate and as the basis for the idealized process of reconciliation with her abusive husband (discussed
further in Chapter 3).

The official psychological report further certified that Marisol had actively engaged with the judicially prescribed therapeutic process, while Gerardo had not. The report states:

> Señora Marisol had a positive attitude toward the therapeutic
> work. In contrast, this same attitude was not observed in Señor
> Gerardo. . . . On the other side, Señora Marisol has remained constant
> in her therapeutic process, which has enabled her to confront
> the relationship with her daughters and the violent situation with
> her husband in a better manner. Currently, she has satisfactorily
> completed her process of personal development in a self-help group
> for family violence, where it has been noted that her self-esteem has
> been reinforced, her social life has been reorganized, and she has
> learned more adaptive ways to resolve conflict. However, it is the
> opinion of the professionals that the achievements made by Señora
> Marisol are hindered by the daily living situation with Señor Gerardo,
> who shows no motivation to change. (official document, September 2,
> 1997)[4]

This information, documented as a technical report and therefore with institutional credibility, was sent to the court. Marisol waited in anticipation for the court's decision to arrive. "Each day of waiting was another day of surviving," she felt.

Over and over again in Marisol's narratives of her experiences with the judicial system, time was a key factor—she was constantly waiting, oftentimes fruitlessly and in terror, for a judicial system response. For Lazarus-Black, in her analysis of the domestic violence law's effects in Trinidad, this manipulation of time is one of a number of "court rites" that "undermine the protective capacity of law" (2007:94). Court rites, she argues, are a vehicle through which the state's interactions with its citizens actually reproduce gendered roles and positions instead of challenging them through the new domestic violence law. Through these court rites, there is an insidious process of silencing, wherein people "are given the opportunity to speak but the content of the message is ignored" (109). In particular, Lazarus-Black identifies "time lags" in the state's responses to women's cases of domestic violence as instrumental in deterring women's persistence in the judicial system. Lazarus-Black posits:

> The conscious and unconscious manipulation of time by various players in the criminal justice system makes it possible, even probable, that in practice, formal legal protection from violence will be obtained only in a small percentage of cases. . . . [O]ver time, these encounters erode the sense of agency and entitlement that bring complainants to court in the first place. . . . [T]hey operate to return the momentary public face of domestic abuse back into the private space of the family. (137–38)

Marisol's daughters suffered through the court system's "time lag" too. "One night," Marisol painfully reminisced,

> they came to my bedroom . . . and they showed me an iron bar that they had hidden underneath my bed, and I asked them what it was for. They told me, "It's for you to defend yourself." And then I said to myself, *Oh my god!* What am I doing to my daughters? What kind of example am I setting for them? I have to fight more strongly to get out of this. It was very painful that they, as adolescent girls, preferred to exercise violence to seeing me in the situation I was in, small and sick. I told them that wasn't necessary, that I was going to do what was necessary, but with the law.

Eventually Marisol tired of waiting and went directly to the courts to inquire, but the clerk told her that she needed a lawyer to receive that information. Marisol told the clerk that she knew that by law she could represent herself, but, Marisol told me, still the clerk denied her the knowledge of what had been decided in her case. Marisol exerted her agency but was denied crucial knowledge that directly impacted her life because she did not have institutionalized, legal authority, and because she did not have the resources to hire a private lawyer. Laws are almost useless without lawyers to aid in the interpretation and use of them, and lawyers cost money. Marisol told me:

From the first hearing, I realized that [the court clerk] was only going
to listen to him. . . . He started telling her things about his intimate life
and his *conquistas amorosas* [romantic conquests], and she examined
him on this in front of me. That irritated me, and I got up and left.
That had nothing to do with anything. She didn't need to ask him
how many women he had had and what he did, and he told her and
all of this happily. . . . *She never protected me.* I take as fact that they
conversed [and] that she must have called the house and told him
what was happening. That's what I think, because how else can I
understand how he hid the notification, and that she didn't give me
any explanation, that they didn't get me a lawyer. (emphasis added)

Soon after, Marisol heard about a toll-free number for complaints of
mishandling of family violence cases. Because of her keen attention
to this innovation in the state's care for women who suffered domestic
violence, she went to the Chilean Ministry of Justice to file a complaint
with the head of the family violence unit about the lack of justice she
had received. There, she learned of the court's verdict, that Gerardo
was to leave their home on September 30, 1997. Of course this verdict
had never arrived. What would have occurred if Marisol had not heard
about the number she could call to protest the mishandling of her
case? What if she had not decided to pursue her case to find out why
she had not received an answer from the court? Marisol felt that her
case simply never would have moved forward. The care she received
was contingent in part on her awareness of laws and mechanisms of the
state and her actions in pursing the care available to her and to which
she felt entitled.

"The clerk had denied me the information," Marisol said. I asked
her how she felt at the time because I wanted to understand more
about how she saw links between the state and her affective experience
(see Jenkins 1991).

"Obviously, I felt that the justice system had not worked the way
it was supposed to," Marisol told me. "I felt humiliated, violated, and,
moreover, vulnerable, because *if the justice system had acted, and the
court hadn't done what the court was supposed to do, what was left? I
didn't have a hope.*"

The Ministry of Justice official to whom Marisol had lodged her complaint told Marisol that she would rectify the situation. She promised to issue another restraining order to oblige Gerardo to vacate their home.

Finally, in March 1998, the Ministry of Justice passed down its decision for a restraining order against Gerardo, stating: "keeping in mind the gravity of the facts and with the goal of guaranteeing the physical and psychological security of the complainant and family it is decreed that entry is prohibited for Sr. Gerardo to the house of the complainant." The restraining order was set for the maximum time of 180 days, and according to the 1994 Family Violence law it could only be renewed if after that time period Gerardo perpetrated another violent act against Marisol or her daughters. Later Marisol learned that Gerardo had received and ignored the notice of the original restraining order in September 1997 and had not told her. Following this 1998 decision by the court, Gerardo moved to Argentina, leaving Marisol to singlehandedly raise their two daughters in the home they owned together. He stayed in Argentina for the following eight years. Marisol had achieved some justice and some peace, but it was temporary.

Conclusions

Marisol's experiences in the judicial system in the years following the Family Violence Law of 1994 reflect those of many of the women I interviewed in 2002 and 2003. Overwhelmingly, the same issues emerged for her as for them: time lags, undue focus on reconciliation, and mistreatment and mishandling of women and their cases.[5] Beyond Marisol's suffering or perhaps because of it, another major thread running throughout the narratives of her life has been her community- and education-oriented outlook and her insistence on fighting for women's rights. Her story has always returned to this, her self-defined "leitmotif." At the same time her narrative has still always been about the suffering she has undergone at Gerardo's hands and how his abuses have been related to the variety of physical and mental health problems she has endured.

Chapter 3 extends Chapter 2's exploration of Marisol's subjectivity in relationship to legal and therapeutic systems, better reflecting the temporal depth inherent in Marisol's lived experiences. Marisol's frustrations with the judicial system only intensified as her odyssey through the system continued following Gerardo's return to Chile in 2006, when she encountered the new Family Violence Law of 2005, the Marriage Law of 2004, the new family courts, and the new judicial system more generally. In Chapter 3 we see how Marisol continued to struggle to use the state's mechanisms for her own purposes and to not be defined or mindlessly "made up" by labels assigned in legal and therapeutic systems. In the process, Marisol's gendered citizenship also emerges more clearly.

CHAPTER 3

"Exhaustion"

Becoming a Victim and a Deserving Citizen

"He came back, *no más, 'po* [just like that]," Marisol told me matter-of-factly in 2009 in the house she rented in a small town near the Chilean coast, about one and a half hours by bus from Santiago. It was situated on a dirt road just beyond where the paved road ended. She pointed my attention to the boarded-up hole in her living room window and to the security bars that cover it. Thieves had entered the window to steal her daughter Paloma's computer that she used for her university studies and to connect to the Internet, a crucial interpersonal and informational link for Marisol as well. Although the area was crime-ridden, Marisol told me that she was not afraid. Marisol was now living here with Paloma because the complaints she filed in the judicial system and the sentences passed down since 1996 had provided her no protection from Gerardo's return in 2006 to the home they owned in Santiago where she had been living for the eight previous years, while he resided in Argentina. Since they remained married and the six-month restraining order from 1998 had run out long ago, he felt entitled to take up residence there again. The house was legally in his name, after all. After his return, Marisol had lived first with her ailing mother, then with her sister and her family, and finally here with Paloma.

This chapter addresses how, in order for women who suffer from gender-based intimate partner violence to seek and claim their rights, the state has made necessary an individualization of those problems. Women must fit themselves into the structures that exist. This individualization, which happens in part through a *bureaucratization of the self*, a process of allowing oneself to be turned into or actively turning oneself into an object of bureaucratic knowledge, can be particularly

detrimental in cases of domestic violence because of its nature as a social, not an individual, pathology.

In this chapter I explore how Marisol's iterative search for care and
her struggle to claim her rights continued after Gerardo's return in
2006, in a shifting legal landscape. She continued to construct a narrative of her experiences in different venues of the state, and she learned
how to arm herself with the bureaucratic traces of her life and suffering
that would support her case to claim her rights as a "victim" of domestic violence and therefore to claim her citizenship.

By 2006 many changes had been made in the judicial landscape
that Marisol now had to navigate. Women's rights sectors continued to
push reform of key legal structures. In 2005 they succeeded in shifting
legal structures when the congress approved reforms to the new Family
Violence Law (Gobierno de Chile 2005a), based on Representatives
María Antonieta Saa and Adriana Muñoz's proposal, drafted in 1999.[1]
One of their critiques of the enactment of the 1994 Family Violence
Law was that "victims repeat their stories many times, have to recover
archived documents, get confused, [face] differential application of
criteria, etcetera, all of which results in inefficient interventions that
are slow and as a consequence do not protect" (Gobierno de Chile
2005a:6–8). Some of Marisol's most frustrating experiences reflected
this critique almost identically. The 1999 report also highlighted the
problematic nature of the 1994 Family Violence Law's emphasis on
reconciliation. Congressional representatives from the right and left
of the political spectrum heralded the reforms enacted in the 2005
Family Violence Law as a key success for women's rights.[2] Representative Adriana Muñoz highlighted the 2005 Family Violence Law's deep
roots in the work of the women's rights movement of the late 1980s and
beyond, noting:

> A very important change has been made in how public policy and the
> laws are made. Issues such as the one we are discussing today used to
> be culturally considered part of private life, intimate . . . but with [the
> Family Violence Law of 1994], they began to form part of the public
> and policy agenda of Chile. It is necessary to highlight the women's
> movement's active participation in striving to publicize the suffering

of thousands of women who endure this scourge and installed the issue in the agenda of the transition to democracy in our country. (Gobierno de Chile 2005a:183)

"This is a very important day for Chilean society, not only for the Chilean woman," proclaimed Representative Isabel Allende, noting the crucial nature of the participation of various Chilean and international women's rights–oriented organizations in the passage of the new law, including Corporación Humanas, DOMOS, the Women's House of Talca, and Amnesty International (Gobierno de Chile 2005a:493). Even conservative Representative Lily Pérez noted, "Each modification to this law . . . without a doubt is a strengthening in women's rights and the Chilean family." Pérez's statement reflects her support of feminist goals, but only insofar as they support women's historically entrenched roles as the moral pillars of "the Chilean family" in its dual sense—both the heterosexual nuclear family and the imagined community of the Chilean nation as a family (see Anderson 1998; Gobierno de Chile 2005a:415–16).

As with the Family Violence Laws of 1994 and 2005, the women's movement and representatives in the congress were instrumental in pushing through the Civil Marriage Law (Ley de Matrimonio Civil, Ley 19.947), passed in 2004 (Gobierno de Chile 2004). This law, which legally recognized divorce for the first time, replaced the Civil Marriage Law of 1884. The debates that surrounded the passage of this law represent the changes related to gender and women's rights that are continuously occurring in the government in the midst of a challenging environment heavily influenced by the power of the Catholic Church's ideals of family. The Catholic Church vehemently opposed the passage of the 2004 Civil Marriage Law, launching a television advertising campaign entitled "Defend the Unity of the Family," claiming that "Chile wants a united family. Let's not divide it."[3] Although the church defended its claims and continued with its campaign for a "united family," the women's movement, NGOs, and many others in society strongly supported the recognition of divorce, which led to the law's passage, but not without concessions. The official rationale for the law echoes the Chilean Constitution of 1980 and ideas of "the family" embedded in the foundations of the Chilean nation. Article 1 of the 2004 Civil Marriage Law affirms, "The family is the fundamental nucleus of society. Marriage is the principal base of the family" (Gobierno de Chile 2004). It requires a three-year waiting period for unilateral divorce and a one-year waiting period for a bilateral divorce. Women's rights advocates fought hard for and won the inclusion of Article 29, which explicitly states that a complaint of family violence constitutes grounds for filing for divorce unilaterally, with a one-year, not three-year, waiting period. The law also pointedly addresses cases of domestic violence by paying special attention to equality between the divorcing partners during processes of mediation. This focus is related to the failure of the Family Violence Law of 1994 to provide for such parity during the reconciliation process, a failure widely understood as having put women at further risk.[4]

By 2006, other major changes had taken place in the Chilean legal system since Marisol had sought help there. Most notably for Marisol, family courts had been instituted and charged to address divorce-related issues, alimony, and noncriminal domestic violence cases. This innovation was part of the broader structural reforms in the Chilean judicial system that occurred during the mid-2000s, when the Ministerio Público (Public Prosecutor's Office) was created. In this new system, cases are adjudicated in public courts and investigated and prosecuted by public officials.

The institutional landscape for women who suffered domestic violence in Marisol's municipality had also shifted by 2006 when she again sought care. The newly elected, politically conservative mayor had instituted the Family Treatment Center, a change that Marisol herself, along with Safe Space and other women's rights organizations, had protested at a public hearing in 2003 (see Chapter 6).[5] In Marisol's experiences from 2006 to 2009, the Family Treatment Center played an important role, at least in documenting and providing institutional credibility for her suffering to the state via the judicial system. Safe Space was no longer offering therapy or judicial assistance and had largely shifted its agenda to research and training. It had relocated to a different municipality of Santiago, in part because of municipal funding cuts that channeled resources away from feminist-centered domestic violence services to the mayor's Family Treatment Center.

"Scientific" Proof: From Invisible, Private Suffering to Documented Public Truth

In 2009 Marisol talked about being keenly aware of her need to prove her institutional credibility and visibility in the eyes of the state's juridical and medical structures as she struggled for her house after Gerardo's return. The family violence bureaucracy and the judicial system forced her *once again* to prove her credibility as a "victim of family violence" in order to successfully file for divorce and to request alimony and other reparations from Gerardo. Marisol was forced to claim her victimhood in order to claim her rights from the state and in her intimate relationship. She gathered copious documentation to submit to the courts as "proof" of what she had suffered; this "proof" included letters from civic organizations where she played leadership roles, domestic violence court-related documents, and psychological evaluations from various institutions. Again, in this process, Marisol was both refuting and embodying the role of the "victim," and she was claiming a particularly gendered relationship to the state and, thereby, a novel form of gendered citizenship. When I was with her in 2009, I asked whether she would be interested in sharing some of these documents with me. She scanned and e-mailed me approximately fifty documents, which constitute traces of the processes through which Marisol's subjectivity was categorized by juridical, medical, and psychological officials. Her knowledge of what happened to her was turned into various technical documents, legible within the bureaucratic structures of the state. In order to claim her rights, this is what she was forced to do.

In July 2006, upon Gerardo's return to their home in Santiago, Marisol, again armed with knowledge of the judicial system and a sense of her rights, continued to refuse to succumb to Gerardo's abuses of power in their relationship. She proudly told me that she had "never spent a day in bed crying."

She went almost immediately to her municipality's mental health clinic (Centro de Salud Mental, or COSAM) to seek help, where she received psychological therapy for several months. A "psychological report" they produced on her behalf, which she submitted to the courts as "proof" of her case in the form of professionalized, authoritative knowledge (Sargent and Bascope 1996), states:

> Señora Marisol entered the mental health program this year, presenting with symptoms such as emotional anguish [*angustia*], rage, emotional lability, among others. The patient associates these symptoms with the arrival of her husband on July 15th of this year at their home, who in March 1998 left with a judicial order for family violence. Additional to this, the patient's mother passed away at the end of October this year, which augmented the symptoms already present in the patient.
>
> The patient, who continues in therapy to the present moment, is diagnosed with "Anxious-Depressive Adaptive Disorder" [*Trastorno Adaptivo Ansioso-Depresivo*], possibly produced by the presence of her husband, who, according to the patient, continues exercising psychological violence. It is recommended that the patient continue in the mental health program and that legal assistants begin the paperwork for separation and for a Family Violence complaint. (official document, December 26, 2006).

The document referred Marisol to the judicial assistance center (Centro de Asistencia Judicial, or CAJ) to receive assistance because of her history of family violence and Gerardo's recent return to their home in Santiago (official document, July 2006). Marisol went instead in October 2006 to the Family Treatment Center which had in a sense replaced Safe Space, to seek legal support for her divorce. Here, Marisol's agency was shaped by her knowledge of one of the state's new legal mechanisms, the Civil Marriage Law of 2004, commonly known as the divorce law.

In order to take advantage of this new law, Marisol needed free assistance from the judicial assistance center. Without a lawyer to make her case, it was almost worthless to proceed. Again, Marisol's experiential knowledge and suffering paled in comparison to the technical, professionalized knowledge of those who work in the judicial and health care systems. A social worker at the Family Treatment Center provided her with another interinstitutional referral to the judicial assistance center, where she had been referred previously but did not go and went instead back to the Family Treatment Center. In her referral of Marisol to the judicial assistance center for her divorce, the Family Treatment Center social worker noted that Marisol was fifty-four years old and possessed a college degree:

> She has been married for 26 years in a conjugal society regime [i.e., without a prenuptial agreement that goods of the couple will be shared][6], she works as a housewife and gives individual art classes. It's important to highlight that for 8½ years she has been separated in fact from Gerardo, 71 years old, who after living and working in Argentina, returned to Chile to live in the same home that they own.

In order for the social worker at the Family Treatment Center to refer Marisol to the judicial assistance center so that she could petition for a divorce on the grounds of "family violence," Marisol once again had to narrate her suffering. Her processes of care-seeking were painstakingly repetitive and based on bureaucratic exigencies, not on an ethic of care for her suffering. But Marisol at times also seemed to refuse and resist going through the "proper" bureaucratic channels. Here is her experience boiled down into the social worker's documentation of her case:

> She has experienced psychological family violence on the part of her spouse. . . . He yells, demands her attention, controls her, and creates points of conflict that make it intolerable [for them] to live together. She has a history of experiencing Family Violence with previous complaints in the Civil Court of Santiago. Señora Marisol has lived physical, sexual, and psychological family violence [and has received] psychological therapy in institutions such as Safe Space, the Women's

Organization and the Family Treatment Center. (official document, 2006)

Instead of going to the judicial assistance center, however, where both the Family Treatment Center and the local mental health center had referred her for legal aid, Marisol decided to go directly to the Santiago Family Court, armed with these pieces of evidence, to petition for her divorce, alimony, a restraining order against Gerardo, and for him to leave their home. The family court was opened in 2005 as part of the overall judicial reforms undertaken in Chile in order to modernize their legal system.[7] Marisol did not understand or did not wish to use the proper channels within this system in order to have her "proof" of suffering heard. At the family court, she told me, they asked for her history in the judicial system. She explained to them, she said, that she had filed many complaints and that Gerardo had been remiss in his duties because he had gone to Argentina for eight and a half years, where he was effectively immune from any attempt she might have made to obtain his support for herself and her daughters.

Marisol went to the family court in Santiago accompanied by a friend, because, she explained to me, "Once you . . . sign the papers . . . you start to question if you were fair." I assumed, based on this statement, that she meant that she wanted her friend to be there with her for moral support. However, when I asked Marisol if she wanted her friend's support in case she wavered in her resolve to file the papers against Gerardo, Marisol expressed another facet of her leitmotif, of her desire to fight for herself and for other women who also lived intimate violence. She explained: "What I wanted was not for her to evaluate me to see if I had acted fairly. What I wanted was for her to learn, because she was in the same situation, so that she could see that it wasn't hard to get there [to the court]." Her motivations, as she looked back to narrate them to me, had to do with her need for support from her friend. But it also seemed very important for her to make clear to me that her main goal was not to solicit support from her friend but to teach her friend, who was also suffering domestic violence, about her rights and how to use them.

As Marisol narrated her experiences, her actions and interactions were saturated through and through with her creation of meaning and a particular rendition of her subjectivity. Though she was constrained, she was creative in her uses of the systems that she had at her disposal. Strikingly, she was very self-consciously engaged in creating something new in that process. In reading and interpreting her own life with me as the listener, Marisol was constantly using a lens through which she could view herself as an independent, smart, creative, well-informed, and caring person, as an educator to her friends, and as an activist struggling for women's right to live free from violence. Were these thoughts actually running through her mind at the time she engaged with the legal system? This cannot be known; however, this sense of herself—composed of her memories of past actions and interpretations of those actions, her narrative of her life—is what she wanted to share as she talked with me.

Marisol had "asked for a lot things," as she put it, at the family court, and they referred her back, once again, to her municipality's judicial assistance center. This was her third referral there. The official notice of the order from the family court states that the judicial assistance center had to provide "a legal representative to defend Doña Marisol and to counsel her with respect to her rights," to assist her in her petition for "a judicial separation, or divorce, health care, and division of the family's belongings" (official document, November 24, 2006).

Now back at her municipality's judicial assistance center, Marisol was finally assigned to a lawyer whom she trusted. She was appreciative of the affective connection she was able to make with this particular lawyer, who was after all an agent of the state. "She knows how to listen," Marisol told me.

> When I went to talk with her the first time, she told me she completely understood me. . . ."Don't worry. You are a very determined woman. . . . I am going to support you, and I know we're going to win," she told me. Obviously she asked me about my whole story. Since I have everything very well organized, I told her the whole story, quickly. "I am going to support you," she told me. "I am going to be with you. We are going to ask for him to leave the house."

In effect, Marisol made an affective connection with the state through this empathic and competent lawyer, whom Marisol felt actually cared about her well-being. Marisol perceived that her suffering was not only listened to, but heard, and not only heard, but adequately acted upon, to the fullest extent possible.

At the judicial assistance center, Marisol had *once again* given her statement of her suffering. How many times had she remembered and reconstituted the painful events of her life to officials of the state and others, including me? Again and again, I knew.

Marisol was well-practiced at a carefully constructed, coherent, and consistent narrative, which has appeared in various documents and in our conversations over the years. She consistently included testimony of her psychological suffering, as well as reference to the variety of institutions where she had sought help. The following is an excerpt of her narrative as encoded in the judicial assistance center document. This fragment shows how well crafted her narrative had become:

I have suffered physical, sexual, psychological, verbal and economic violence permanently on the part of the defendant . . . [as well as] physical and psychological threats, yelling, belittlement, beatings, nasty words, obsessive control of my personality. . . . [Because of him I] have had to enter numerous therapy programs in institutions like Safe Space, CONFA, and the Women's Organization, in 2003, and the Family Treatment Center and the Mental Health Center in Santiago, during 2006, to in some way be able to overcome the abuses . . .
There is prior documentation of family violence, such as for example, what I declared in my 1996 complaint for violence and in 1997 [and in] March 1998, a restraining order against Gerardo. . . . Also, the violent events have been denounced to the Chilean Police. . . . Since my husband's return from Argentina in July 2006, he has again used violence against my daughter and me, including physical aggression against her, punches, pushing and insults. From November 2006 to the present day I have been permanently exposed to psychological violence consisting of my husband's belittlements of me, such as that I am lazy, uncaring, useless, and a failure; also I have received abuses consisting of slaps [and] bad words, which makes me live in a

constant state of fear for my physical and mental security. In the last act of violence, my husband arrived drunk, with an aggressive attitude, intimidating us, all of which was in addition to his psychological and economic threats that I would end up in the street with nothing, moreover, that he wouldn't provide further for my daughter's education.

In light of the situation that I have just explained, it is impossible for me to maintain a normal relationship in the communal home and my own and my daughter's safety, all of which add to the constant fear in which we live, in addition to being subjected to his attacks of rage and abrupt mood changes, I find it necessary to accuse my husband of Family Violence.

The lawyer from the judicial assistance center took this version of Marisol's narrative and turned it into the legal documents needed to make her case for the state to force Gerardo to leave their home. The document requests the following: "A [court] order for his immediate exit from the communal home and that he be condemned as an author of family violence and condemned to pay 10 UTM as a fine."

Marisol had found a lawyer who could translate her experiences, needs, and desires into language that was intelligible to the legal system and therefore to the state. But Marisol wavered. In 2007 the lawyer at the judicial assistance center filed Marisol's petition, but Marisol requested to retract it after talking with her daughters. She explained that the lawyer had tried to talk her out of retracting the complaint and told her, "Stop thinking about everyone else. Be selfish." But Marisol felt the tug of her daughters' relationship with their father:

I talked to my daughters, and they said . . ."No, you can't do that to dad. We know that he hasn't acted right, that you are right, but it makes us sad for our dad." The younger daughter told me that he is trying. So, you feel like the bad guy [*mala de la película*]. . . . You have taught them. . . . *Claro*, that's the most difficult part. . . . They tell me, "This goes against everything you've taught us. You always told us that our dad . . . that if he was sick, we'd have to give him a hand, and if he was old, we'd have to give him a hand. You . . . take in cats, dogs, people, everybody, and you're going to throw my dad out." And really, you start thinking about it, and darn it, how unjust. . . . The rights of my daughters' father. I had a relationship, anyway, in quotes, *"de amor"* [of love] with him, right?

Here, Marisol laughed ironically at the idea that there had ever really been love between them. She explained her laughter and continued her story: "I say, in quotes, because you realize, after time, that it wasn't love. You know? So, I went and talked with the lawyer again, and she said, 'You will regret it.' And she told me, 'I am going to be here to help you again, when you decide. But, you are wrong,' she said."

Marisol began to cry as she thought about how she had decided not to have the lawyer submit the petition for Gerardo to be ordered out of their home by legal decree. "Time proved her right," Marisol told me. "Because time passed, and I got sick, and just like she said, I am the one who lost," she lamented.

Nevertheless, Marisol continued with her case to request that Gerardo provide for her financially. In a decree from July 9, 2007, and a brief letter dated July 17, 2007, from the family court in Santiago, Marisol received notice that a court date had been set for February 15, 2008, seven months later. This court date was about eighteen months after she first asked the Family Treatment Center for aid to petition for alimony.

Then, in December 2007 Marisol suffered a stroke, which left her speech, memory, and movement affected, but she continued to struggle not just to survive but for a meaningful life. In 2009, I visited the public health center where Marisol spent a lot of her time after her stroke, in the occupational therapy unit. There, a Japanese therapist on an exchange program taught her techniques, including origami, for recovering her manual and cognitive abilities. Marisol walked me by the occupational therapy wing of the health center while we were there for a dental emergency that had arisen for her the morning of my arrival. She showed me the beautiful and intricately complex origami pineapple and lobster she had made under the therapist's tutelage. Soon, she said, she would teach others how to make origami figures at a community fair. Through this program, she was able to make new connections with people, as she had in programs for domestic violence in the past. These experiences were all marked by the forging of new biosocial relationships, new kinships of affliction and affinity (see Rapp 1999). It helped that Marisol was a "good patient," that is, a patient who was able and willing to engage fully in her treatment course (see Biehl 2007). She also knew how to take advantage of services, as well as new forms of biosociality, available to her.[8]

Marisol made claims based on the trauma she experienced, related to Gerardo's violence against her but also related to her ongoing health difficulties, including her recent stroke. In preparation for her February 15, 2008, court date Marisol carefully documented her expenses and necessities in the aftermath of her stroke, noting, "I do not add to the family income because I have been out of work due to a stroke suffered in December 2007, from which I am recuperating." She requested that Gerardo, as her husband, pay her a monthly pension in order to cover the following (currency amounts are given in Chilean pesos):

Cymbalta:	$19,400 (a common antidepressant)
Somazina:	$20,000 (for brain damage caused by her stroke)
Omeprazol:	$2,800 (generic of Prilosec, for reflux)
Tensodox:	$4,800 (skeletal muscle relaxant)
Other:	$18,000
Special Nutritional Needs:	$30,000
Neurological Exams (2):	$17,000
Mammogram:	$12,000
Clothing:	$15,000
Cleaning Products:	$10,000
Telephone:	$5,000
Transportation:	$23,400
Total Expenses:	$177,400 (about US$350)

Marisol's detailed claims, along with her other documents, were sent to the family court in anticipation of the hearing for family violence scheduled for February 15, 2008.

Psychiatric Evaluations as Proof

The day of the hearing in the family court finally arrived. Marisol was granted a provisional alimony order for Gerardo to pay her 40 percent of the monthly minimum wage (Chilean pesos $57,600; around US$115). This was about two-thirds less than she had requested to cover her basic necessities and medications; however, this amount, when combined with her disability pension from the state and her daughter's contributions to the rent and household they shared, allowed Marisol to barely cover her most urgent necessities. She also received a restraining order against Gerardo, and the judge ordered both Marisol and Gerardo to undergo psychiatric evaluation at the mental health center or the juridical medical service, as they had done more than ten years earlier, in 1997. The objective was to ascertain whether "the defendant fits the characteristics of an abuser and if the plaintiff has been a victim of family violence" (official document, February 15, 2008). A court date for four months later was set for a review of the psychological evaluations and other evidence.

In May 2008, a social worker in her municipality's Office of Matters of Family and Disability conducted Marisol's psychological evaluation, as ordered by the family court. On the official document the social worker noted the goal: "to detect the presence of *symptoms* associated with Family Violence" (emphasis added). Family violence in this official state document has "symptoms," as though it is a sickness, or a pathology, that resides in the individual body and must be dealt with in terms of the individual's symptomatology (see Biehl and Moran-Thomas 2009). Marisol's experience had to be objectified and thereby made credible through the process of certifying that she had telltale "symptoms" of family violence, in the form of psychological traces of past traumas (see Fassin and Rechtman 2009; Herman 1992; Lock 2008; Lock and Nguyen 2010; Young 1995).[9]

The social worker conducted a clinical interview with Marisol and gave her a Rorschach test to evaluate her "symptoms" of family violence (see Table 1). There, Marisol's psychological suffering, her interior mind, was transformed into Xs on a page. The social worker concluded: "Marisol presents the highlighted symptoms associated with psychological abuse generated by the relational dynamic established with her husband" (official document, Office of Matters of Family and Disability, May 2008). The social worker based her evaluation in part on a Rorschach test, an outdated psychological evaluation; nevertheless, Marisol had now, *again*, been officially "diagnosed." Her testimony of her experience had become positive "evidence" of her suffering in the eyes of the state. It was more clearly legible now that it had been turned into an object that the state could recognize as truth. Marisol's knowledge of her experiences on its own was not authoritative. It had to once again be filtered through a professional in order to be considered "truth." In this way, Marisol again and again became a citizen-subject legible to the state, her gendered citizenship revolving around the enactment of her role as a victim of domestic violence.

For Marisol this was *un desgaste*, an exhausting effort, "another time of entering into the same interrogations, to remember the same things. . . . Plus, I was in a disadvantageous situation. I wasn't in my own house. I was living with my sister. Already, the situation wasn't normal," she told me. Marisol expressed the trouble she felt at being probed in this way, of having to prove that she indeed had suffered. She found it demoralizing and degrading to be "judged" in these ways by a stranger, someone she felt was an incompetent official of the state that she no longer trusted to care for her. But what other option did she have than to keep trying to prove to that very state that she had suffered domestic violence?

On June 23, 2008, Gerardo, still living in their Santiago home, went to his municipality's Family Treatment Center for his psychological evaluation, as ordered by the court. The psychologist certified that he angered easily and likely did abuse Marisol psychologically and emotionally. She noted that Gerardo was consumed by the desire for social climbing and status, and that he had been raised within both

Basic personality dimensions	Diminished	Moderate	Average	Above average	Prominent
Emotional stability					
Affective maturity					
Impulse control					
Indicators of depression					
Anxiety					
Relationship with support networks					
Self-esteem					
Submissive/dependent behavior					
Self-assurance					
Ability to make decisions					

Table 1. Official document, Office of Matters of Family and Disability, May 2008

a society and a family where performance of *machista* roles was valorized. The psychologist noted:

> *Machismo* is observed . . . as one of the *aggravating factors* in the deterioration of the relationship. . . . His infidelities and the inequality of rights to which he tried to submit *su mujer* [his woman] . . . in his attempts to exercise the role of father, husband, and partner,

came from demands that the other owes him obedience, setting up a relationship of submission and inequality of rights. [This is] clearly a dynamic of gender violence, in which he is responsible for wanting to maintain a relationship of submission and inequality with *su mujer* [his woman].

She described Gerardo as "a subject with propensities to lose control in situations in which his status as male, 'man of the house,' or 'provider' seem threatened" (official document, June 23, 2009). The psychologist situated his aggression within societal norms and values of *machismo*. Gerardo, the report implied, also recognized his own *machista* values, though he had difficulty recognizing why they were wrong.

I remembered when I read this part of the documentation of her case that Marisol had once told me: "With all of the beauty and wealth we have in this country, we should be living in a paradise. But we're not, because *machismo* is rooted in the culture, in the daily chores. *Machismo* is rooted in daily life."

Many women feel the paradigm of *machismo* in their daily lives (Parson 2012). During one of our group interviews, several women who had been members of the group therapy sessions I observed at Family Care in 2003 discussed how they thought about *machismo*. They said:

Our culture still says that the man should be *machista*. That myth still exists, that the man should be the one to give the orders in the household.

Machismo. . . . It is as if only men have the right to everything and women no, for the fact of being a woman. A man, because he is a man, cannot be washing the plates. The man, because he is a man, cannot take care of babies. Women take care of the children. Something like that, as if the woman takes on everything for the fact of being a woman. [The man says,] "I'm a man. I can't be sweeping." That is *machismo*. They stop being men if they are seen washing plates. They stop being men if they are seen taking care of a baby. . . . Although it is changing a little, bit by bit.

I think that that is the biggest mistake that all men commit. They think that because one gets married one is then their property and one has to do what they want. That is what they do not understand.

The thing is that here men, married men, it is like they are one's owners. One belongs to them, but they do not belong to one, by right. . . . Because of the role.

Chilean scholars have come to similar conclusions about the pervasiveness of *machismo* in Chilean society. Chilean anthropologists Montecino and Acuña (1996:33) have argued that masculinity, dating from the colonial conquest of Spanish invaders over the indigenous population, is imagined as "powerful and violent: the leader [*el caudillo*], the military man, the warrior." Recently, in a 2008 report, "Women's Perceptions of Their Situations and Conditions of Life in Chile," conducted by Corporación Humanas (2008:115), 89 percent of women surveyed throughout Chile said that Chile is a *machista* country. More specifically, 86 percent of women reported that there is sex-based discrimination against women in Chile, and 58 percent of women reported that this discrimination causes women discomfort in *everyday life* (111). When asked where sexist discrimination occurs, 92 percent of women said at work, 60 percent in the family, and 66 percent in political spheres (112).

It was within these wider contexts of sexism that Marisol struggled to achieve justice for herself. On the day of the hearing at the family court in Santiago, Marisol's report from the social worker in her small, coastal town had not yet arrived. "In spite of the fact that I had repeatedly asked the social worker here, the psychologist, to send it on time and give me a copy to take with me, well, it didn't happen," Marisol bitterly complained. She attributed this failure to her feeling that the town where she lived now, outside of Santiago, was very "country," and she noted that officials in the country are "more limited" and less efficient than those in Santiago.

When they finally had the hearing, with Marisol's psychological evaluation as proof, the family court judge classified Marisol's case as "habitual abuse," a new categorization available under the 2005

Family Violence Law.[10] Habitual abuse is loosely defined as either psychological or physical abuse that persists over time and is deemed to be severe because of its long-term nature. I interviewed three public prosecutors in Santiago in June 2009 and was told that the application of the Family Violence Law of 2005 has been contingent on the prosecutors' and judges' interpretations of the law. In particular, they have largely been responsible for defining the ramifications of habitual abuse on a case-by-case basis, and very few sentences have been passed down on that category of crime. Since habitual abuse must be investigated and tried by public prosecutors, family court judges are "incompetent" to hear such cases.

A Family Care lawyer, an expert in representing and counseling women who have suffered domestic violence, explained to me in 2009 that "family court judges . . . didn't want to end up with the family violence cases" and would therefore "declare themselves incompetent and send everything to the prosecutor."

"Women receive more of what they really need in the family court?" I asked her, to clarify.

"We have always had to find a way to trick the system," she told me. Now lawyers who worked with domestic violence cases simply had to devise new ways of "gaming" the system, the lawyer revealed. "I am convinced that the family [court] can do much more than the prosecutor's office. I have to say to the woman, '*Señora*, file a complaint about the last episode. Don't talk about your history.'"

It is better, she explained, to keep cases that are marked by continuous abuse, but that are not physically grave, in the family court. If a woman who suffered domestic violence lacks documentation of physical damage, she can achieve very little with the public prosecutor, even with the classification of habitual abuse. The public prosecutors are powerless to address the range of pressing and "ordinary" issues that often plague these women, such as child support, which have to be addressed in the family court. The public prosecutors I interviewed in 2009 agreed with the Family Care lawyer's assessment that as an institution they are limited to addressing the technical, legal dimensions of family violence cases, which only constitute a small part of the solution in most cases of domestic violence against women. She explained:

The reality is very hard to confront from the criminal context. Because the *Señora* comes with a mountain of problems, and when she finally comes to the criminal system, it's because she wants them to fix everything because she has put up with it for so many years in silence. . . . But that is completely beyond the realm of possibilities, the power. . . . This is what we have been seeing.

The public prosecutors I interviewed in their Santiago high-rise office building in 2009 explained that another problem with classifying women's cases as habitual abuse is that for many women the history of abuse has been so long that remembering precise dates and incidents is almost impossible. It is not uncommon, one of the prosecutors said, to have cases where the prosecutors have difficulty because the "victim can't tell exactly [when the abuses occurred]." "It's very difficult," she said. Actually "proving" the abuse, producing physical evidence, is even more challenging. Another problem, they told me, is that any habitual abuse prior to the enactment of the Family Violence Law of 2005 is not punishable under that law. Therefore, if a woman tells the prosecutor that she has been abused since the couple was dating and throughout their twenty-year marriage, only the abuse after 2005 can be "counted" as evidence of habitual abuse. "That's an issue," she said.

Another major issue identified by both the Family Care lawyer and the public prosecutors is the scarcity of resources and training to adequately *implement* the new laws within the new legal systems. These innovations in the legal system included the new Family Violence Law, the Civil Marriage Law (Divorce Law), and the overhaul of the entire judicial system to an oral system, with a dedicated Family Court.

"It has to do . . . with this underdeveloped society," said one of the prosecutors. "Some decisions tend to mix with the consideration of other elements. . . . It is very difficult for the judges to send a person to jail."

"Why?" I wondered aloud.

The prosecutor explained to me that it was related to a broader, society-wide lack of resources that judges confront in practice. She noted that judges sometimes find in favor of the abuser because if a guilty sentence is passed, the "reality of our country" will also punish the woman who is abused and her children. That is, if the abusive man is jailed, the reality that only about one-third of women do remunerated work (SERNAM 2004a:94) will dictate that the woman and her children will often also lose. "We are continuously looking for a solution," she said.

Similarly, the Family Care lawyer reflected on the problem of a lack of resources:

> We put ourselves in the judge's place, taking into account the reality of our country, which is the other element that they are always considering. And they are presented with a man after committing the act of violence, a woman who in the end warps her version to protect him and says that he's in rehabilitation for alcoholism, that he has found work. . . . The judges think that the problem is under control, without realizing that treatments for alcoholism can fail. . . . They [the judges] are thinking that if they give a criminal sentence, they will throw him out of work. [What about] the family, the children? That is also the reality of this country. . . . To confront the phenomenon of retraction we could shorten investigations, but that wouldn't solve the *Señora's* problem.

The public prosecutor explained that they also often lack human resources to adequately investigate charges. A SERNAM official I interviewed echoed some of these frustrations, explaining: "It's difficult to obtain resources. . . . Here in this country . . . we have advanced in confronting [various] aspects of the problem of gender violence. [However] . . . there is always a lack. It is always insufficient. We know that." The Family Care lawyer concurred: "We always bump up against the resources of the system. This country always has that problem."

Another major problem with the 2005 law and the concomitant judicial system reforms is that many women do not know how to use the judicial mechanisms to their advantage. Many do not seem to understand that the public prosecutors are dedicated to criminal cases, not to divorce and other needs, which are covered in the family courts.

One of the public prosecutors I interviewed illustrated this with a vignette:

> There are women who come to the public prosecutor [i.e., in criminal
> court], who are beaten, threatened and abused. . . . We operate
> in a criminal context. But the woman says, "I just want the public
> prosecutor to see me for a divorce. I would like them to work on
> alimony, visitation rights." . . . So, there, a whole problem is created.
> Because the public prosecutors tell her, "*Señora*, I don't know how to
> do that. That is the charge of the family court."

This misunderstanding by women who suffer domestic violence about how to use the new law, the new family courts, and the public prosecutor can lead to other problems. A SERNAM official told me in 2009 that among the public prosecutors, "We still find ourselves with many functionaries who do not understand the issue. They say, 'Oh no, here comes *that* woman' [i.e., a woman who does not understand the system]. But they are taking steps to train people. The Ministry of the Interior has prosecutors specialized in family violence." Here the lack goes beyond the material resources to a lack of understanding and cultural shifts in the judicial system.

At any rate, now that Marisol's case had been classified as habitual abuse, which defined it as a criminal case, it was with the public prosecutor's office and therefore no longer under the jurisdiction of the judicial assistance center. However, the judicial assistance center lawyer and her intern, with whom Marisol had made an affective connection, insisted on maintaining their involvement in the case anyway. Marisol knew a lot of her rights, aspects of the law, and the legal system. She is well-spoken and intelligent, and I speculate that all of this made her a "good client" for the system, perhaps making it more likely for her to receive extraordinary support (cf. Merry 2006).

After she had waited for what she felt was a "prudent time" to hear about a resolution to her case from the prosecutor, Marisol called in November 2008 to inquire about its status. They informed her that the case had been archived. She asked how that could be and why she had never received notifications. They told her that they had sent the no-tifications to her home in Santiago where she no longer resided and where Gerardo, against whom she had filed this very complaint, was living.

Marisol became very animated, passionate, and angry in her tone as she narrated this part of her experience to me.

"I was very irritated because I felt that the prosecutors hadn't done their work. Because it can't be that they receive a file with the whole story, and they can't read it to see where the victim lives, because that's the *most minimal*. Because who should they worry about the most? *The victim*" (emphasis added).

I interjected, "But this is a case of family violence, even though the law has changed—" She continued the thread:

> The law has changed. . . . It's obvious that it's necessary for people to have to apply criteria. For me, they didn't use the criteria. Because if they are seeing a case of VIF [*Violencia Intrafamiliar*, or family violence], as you said, it's obvious that they won't be [living] together, even more if it is a housing-related order. What are the lodging arrangements? Where is she? Where is he? Right?

The judicial officials had sent the notification to the wrong address, and if Marisol had not followed up, she never would have known. Upon learning this, Marisol went to the prosecutor to talk to the per-son in charge of her case. "She asked me a lot of questions," she said. "Later I understood that I was filing *another* complaint. But I didn't know I was filing another complaint. And all of the other papers had been moved . . . the whole file."

There, they gave her a new court order to give to Gerardo. She was in Santiago at that time to go to their house to pick up some of her work things. "My paints, my tools, my kiln," she told me. "That, I still haven't been able to bring because it is undergoing repair in Santiago. Soon I'll get it back, and that will be a tool for working. Once I have the kiln, I'll be able to give pottery classes and other things." Marisol had planned the trip to her Santiago home at that time because she knew Gerardo would not be there, so she agreed to take the new court order from the prosecutor to Gerardo. She refused the police escort that the court had mandated was her due because she did not want to put on a "show" for her neighbors. She instead went with a friend. She explained, "If I had gone with the police, I would have done him [Gerardo] huge damage because he works from home. I would have done him great economic harm, moral damage, maybe psychological damage. I don't know if it would have affected him or not, but I didn't want that." Harm to him could also represent harm to herself. If he suffered economic damages, for example, she could also, as she was in part dependent on the money he had to send her.

Marisol described for me, through tears and a wavering voice, how it felt for her to return to their home.

> I was really bad, when I entered my house, when I saw the conditions that my house was in, everything poorly cared for, the garden dead, the plants horrible, a filth, that no one had cleaned at all . . . all of my things, thrown around, abandoned, on the patio, the kitchen table, thrown around. It was very painful for me to see my house abandoned like that. I cried a lot. I went with a friend, to organize all of my things to take with me, but I cried a lot, a lot of sadness.

At this point in our conversation, in the middle of bites of crunchy Chilean *marraqueta* (a popular type of bread), Marisol glanced around her living room and signaled with her hands for me to me to look around for myself. "In this house, there is nothing from there," she told me.

Finally, Marisol received her court date via certified mail at her address in the small town where she and Paloma lived. The order told her to appear in the court, though they did not specify which one, she told me, and they did not tell her it was in the criminal court (Juzgado de Garantía). Marisol had the impression that she should go to the court she was already familiar with, the family court, but this was incorrect. Hers was now a criminal case. "So, it was time [for the hearing to start], and I had to fly there with my friend who was accompanying me," she

Figure 1. Looming in the distance is the new judicial center. (Photograph by the author, 2009)

said, because she had first gone to the family court, which was the wrong location. When Marisol, supported as she often was by a friend, finally entered the correct courtroom in the criminal court, she said that Gerardo was already sitting there and the hearing had begun without her.

On the advice of the lawyer at the Santiago SERNAM Women's Center in 2009, I had already spent two days at the criminal court, observing various proceedings. I noted, upon arriving at the judicial center for the first time, how it looms large on the skyline (see Figures 1, 2, and 3). Gigantic, sleek, and modern, it had been completed in 2006 to house the reformed court system that now included public courtrooms.

Once inside, I found my way up the glass elevators to a lovely courtroom, where several family violence cases were being heard. It was lined with hardwood walls and benches for audience members—all very formal and seemingly with lavish investment. The family violence cases comprised only a fraction of all of the cases being publicly adju-

Figure 2. The hypermodern judicial center. (Photograph by the author, 2009)

Figure 3: A building near the new judicial center. The graffiti in the center, of the man in glasses, is of deposed president Salvador Allende. (Photograph by the author, 2009)

dicated in the same session. There were also cases of pirated CD sales and supermarket thefts, for example. A woman I spoke with while we waited for the court to open told me she was there because her son had been picked up by police because he was caught carrying a pocket knife to defend himself. She said, "In the *población* [poor neighborhood/shantytown] even little kids have to carry arms." The state invests so much in disciplining the poor. The family violence cases were not all male partners against women victims; one was a fight between a woman and her brother-in-law.

The defendants filed into the room as a group, and the plaintiffs waited in the audience until it was their turn to sit next to the prosecutor, who argued their cases. I sat at the back of the room on a bench with a woman and her son, who was probably six years old. He was squirmy, so I dug into my bag and pulled out a pen, paper, and some stickers from the notebook where my daughter had been drawing earlier that day and offered them to him. He happily accepted and began drawing; his rather distraught-looking mother smiled gratefully to me. Toward the end of the session, her case was called, and she proceeded to the front of the room while her son stayed on the bench next to me, listening. The facts of her case were read, and I realized that hers was a family violence case. The prosecutor, whom the woman had just met, read in monotones from the file. Her husband had threatened to kill her with a knife. The boy, who remained seated to my left, leaned over and whispered to me, "That's my father. He threatened my mother with a knife," as he performed a stabbing motion in the air between us. The woman was asking for a restraining order, but also for her husband to be ordered into treatment for his alcoholism. The judge handed down the sentence, a restraining order for thirty days. The Prosecutor countered by asking for forty-five days, which the judge denied. The final outcome at this stage was that the husband was restricted from coming near her and/or their home for thirty days. He was also on probation for one year, which meant that if he again abused her he would be subject to jail and further penalties. When the court adjourned, this woman made her way out, and we locked eyes. I asked her what she thought about the sentence. She said, with tears brimming, that she just wanted him to get treatment for alcoholism. He refused to recognize his problem with alcohol, she said. She told me that her case would now go for investigation, and hopefully they would eventually send him to treatment.

I reflected on my observations as I listened to Marisol describe her experiences in the criminal court. Marisol's case was in the same building in the sleek new judicial center but was up a level from the court I had seen. Her case had already been sent to the prosecutor for investigation, where the woman I spoke with in the courtroom would proceed next. Marisol described the courtroom scenario when she finally arrived in the right place, which was in the new judicial center: "He was there with his lawyer. There were two or three other people. I don't know who they were, the team in front, my lawyer, whom I didn't know, and my friend." She had never met her lawyer before, which meant that she did not know ahead of time the declaration on which her case was based. "I didn't like that one bit," she told me. "I sent an e-mail to ask them to send it to me [and to say] that I wanted to be in contact with the prosecutor or the lawyer, and I never was able." Then, she told me about the situation in the court:

> I enter, and the lawyer turns around and says to me—I'll tell you right away, this seemed really harsh to me—I enter. He turns around. He stands up, and he says to me, "You are Señora Marisol?" "Yes," I tell him. Then he says, "Señora Judge, she is the Señora. She is the *victim*," he says to her. Oy! That for me was very harsh . . . I felt like. . . . It's like when you see a sign that says "*buscado*" (wanted). You understand? *They didn't have any reason to call me the victim, because when I hear that word in front of him I feel lesser.*

The judge ordered a one-year restraining order for Gerardo. This would have been impossible under the 1994 version of the law, which allowed for only up to 180 days for a restraining order. When I interviewed Marisol in June 2009 she was in the middle of this one-year period. She still did not want to use the restraining order to uproot Gerardo from their shared home in Santiago. The Santiago family court sent a certified letter to Marisol on January 13, 2009, which set a court date for April 23, 2009, to address her appeal for more alimony. Mari-

sol, with the support of the two lawyers and a judicial system mediator, negotiated for Gerardo to pay her a monthly pension of 60 percent
of the minimum wage, which works out to be approximately $100,000
Chilean pesos per month (approximately US$185). Marisol is very
conscious of her situation in relation to Gerardo's. She feels that he has
great advantages over her financially, largely because he is the one who
remains in the couple's home but also because he worked consistently
for money. Marisol told me:

> You have to think about the economic damage he has done to me.
> He received his pension from Argentina, an excellent pension, and
> he spent it all by himself. He didn't give anything to me, and I have a
> right because I am his wife. That's what the law says. . . . He was in a
> privileged situation. Not me. I don't have any income. I don't have my
> networks. I don't have my friendships. I don't have my personal things.
> Even my pets are there. Even that is a loss for me, because the pets
> become part of the family.

Marisol also received a disability pension from the state because of
her diagnosis of Thomsen's disorder. Again, she had presented her papers to apply for that pension, another instance in which she knew the
channels through which to work the state to her advantage. By 2009,
with the pension from the state and from Gerardo, Marisol was able
to support herself though did not have enough resources to live alone.

Complications, subtleties, and unknowns are part of life, and this
was not lost in Marisol's experience. She was not forced to leave the
couple's home. She "chose" to do so because she felt that she could
not live there with Gerardo. Marisol told me that she planned to continue pulling the judicial system levers, this time to file for divorce,
when the time became ripe. Once again, she did not only know and
talk about her rights—Marisol was also constantly *mobilizing* to *claim*
those rights. She told me:

> The law now says that divorce can be unilateral, and in my case, where
> there are antecedents of violence, he does not have a leg to stand on.
> In my case I can claim VIF [family violence] and get a divorce. We

don't need the three years [waiting period before divorce, mandated by the Civil Marriage Law of 2004], the one year of separation, or any of that. But the lawyer told me that I shouldn't do it now. "We're going to wait for two years, and when he has just a bit left to pay on the mortgage, then we're going to get him out of the house. Because then," she told me, "You will figure out how to finish paying the mortgage and enjoy your house, *'po.*" I told her that the thing is that I have no love for that house now.

Although she may not "have love for that house now," Marisol has a vision for her future there. She plans to rent out the two upstairs bedrooms to generate extra income. "My dream," she said, "is to be independent. I want live alone. I have my independent airs."

This is another recurrent theme in Marisol's narrative, that she is independent, which is all the more important for her, it seems, because of the various ways she has been *forced to be dependent.* Marisol does not want to continue to live with her daughter.

Critical Thought as Agency and Resilience

Although Marisol has seen a lot of positive changes in the judicial system, she remains critical of many aspects of her experience within that system. She told me that she is collecting all of the information about her experiences so that she can write a letter to various governmental and nongovernmental officials, including María Antonieta Saa on the Commission on the Family in the House of Representatives, House Representative María Angelica Cristi, SERNAM, and Safe Space. Marisol shared one of her suggestions with me:

The victims of the dictatorship have a card that they present. Why can't we, as victims of violence, show an identification card? For that [purpose] they have made that card [for dictatorship victims], so that people don't have to give explanations repeatedly. Also, the people who work on this problem and have passed laws about this problem, this hasn't happened to them. They haven't had to live this, this going around, going and coming, going and coming. They haven't been in the role of victim, thank God. Luckily they haven't been, but because of that I think it's important for them to have empathy and be able to put themselves into someone else's place or, as I say, stand up to life from the front, to see it.

She identified here the disjuncture between discourses, laws, institutions, and media dealing with family violence, the realities of the women who suffer this violence, and the difficulties they face in having their complicated needs met. At this point in the conversation, I observed—based on what Marisol had been expressing to me, as well as what I know of her from our friendship for the past six years—that for the past fourteen years she was always attentive to the laws and had won a lot, yet still had to fight *constantly*.

She explained: "Exactly. For me this has been a constant fight. [But] it's not just a constant fight. . . ." Here, she carefully chose the word that would express her overall interior experience. "It's a wearing down [*un desgaste*]," she told me. "It's a very big wearing down [*un desgaste muy grande*], a psychological wearing down." She expressed her inner world of feeling worn down, a feeling of being at wit's end and completely worn out, through and through.

She continued, "The thing is that getting healed [*curarse*] from this is very slow. . . . I think that if there were conversation groups [*talleres de conversación*] and all of that, it would be easier to recover."

Although she had never achieved what she felt she deserved through the judicial system, Marisol explained to me that for her, thinking critically about life, being observant and analytical, allows her to feel free.

It's the freedom to be many things at once, to be a woman, mother, wife, to be a friend, see that you are inserted into a society in which you also have roles you have to fulfill, certain aspects of being a mother and a wife, and that's the freedom that one doesn't have. And I think that if the woman feels that she can't do that, she has to develop it. If not, it's taking out of you your essence as a person. I don't see myself as a woman who is furniture. I don't see myself as an object, in the sense that I am there to attend to a man and to be a mother, and to be an incubator, who has children, nothing more. I see myself beyond that. I see myself as a part of the society. I need the society, the same as the society needs me.

Marisol's narratives of her experiences, thoughts, and forms of resilience are infused with her up-to-date knowledge about the judicial system, based on her own firsthand experience, and also her avid attention to current events and news. In her narratives she is always conscious of these larger structures, as well as the bearing they have on her innermost life world. The judicial system changes and her knowledge of them have become important for her agency and sense of herself. She told me in 2009:

> I continue to have dreams. I have recuperated that capacity to continue having dreams and realize them, even though it's little by little. It's obvious that it's going to be more difficult than when I was young. But basically, for a bad choice, a bad decision, a lot of things were frustrated. That's what I think. With all of these new laws, all of these things also are going to be possible. And also that the society learns to see women from a different perspective. That she can. We have to give her opportunities. She doesn't have to be marked by the violence, because still, although there's a law, we are very marked. It really bothers me. Happily, last year I didn't have to do it, but for years I had to go in front of a notary to declare that I was allowed to use the house, property that wasn't mine legally, for financial gain. Because I was married I had rights to that house [but] I wasn't the owner. So for example, that's a part of the law that's broken.

Conclusions

Beginning in 1996, Marisol constantly attempted to mobilize various resources of the state, in addition to nongovernmental resources like Safe Space, to confront and escape abuse. As of 2009, her processes of seeking help in the judicial system had lasted for fourteen years and had been shaped over time by various changes in state-level laws, policies, and practices. Her efforts to achieve justice and a better life for herself had been iterative, circular, and continuous. This was clear in 2003 when Marisol first narrated her experiences to me and has become only more apparent over time.

Marisol's experiences bring to light that the postauthoritarian, neoliberal, ostensibly gender-sensitive state, while providing some structural possibilities for and certainly a discursive construction of gender equality, has failed in many women's views to bring these promises to *practice*. Women who are abused, with low self-esteem and in dangerous situations, oftentimes must activate the state's mechanisms *over and over again* — Marisol continued to do so for fourteen years and continues still. Her interactions with the judicial system have been at once empowering and absolutely frustrating. The iterative, never-ending process of going back and forth to various institutions of the state, always fighting for her rights, has *worn her down*. The state is therefore both active and passive in its offering of citizenship — and it thereby creates a gendered form of citizenship for some of its members. Biehl (2007) describes the importance of AIDS sufferers' personal responsibility for seeking help, asserting their "will to live," and being "good patients." This notion of personal responsibility lies at the crux of the neoliberal ideology about citizenship (Merry 2006; Ong 2006). Others who cannot achieve this level of self-efficacy, this ability to seek and demand help from the state and then behave "properly" in those help-giving institutions, are cast out or socially abandoned (Biehl 2005). In effect this is a moral system wherein only certain kinds of certifiable "victims" are able to access justice, or some modified version thereof. In the case of domestic violence, the majority of sufferers are female, which thus implies a form of gendered citizenship.

The difficulties Marisol faced in accessing the laws of the state, ostensibly designed to protect her, not only reinforced but became *part of* that domestic violence and the ongoing suffering it produced. Her experience shows how the state's laws, policies, and actions are embedded within intimate relationships, acting to perpetuate gender inequality and intimate gender violence against women. In her narrative rendition of her life, Marisol describes how her subjectivity has been interrelated with psychological, psychiatric, and judicial systems, run largely through the state, as well as with Safe Space and other women's rights programs. She has constantly mobilized the tools the state offered her in her ongoing struggle to assert her agency, though that agency has always been constrained (see Stark 2007). State and affect were linked in Marisol's experience in novel ways, and this linkage points to a form of gendered citizenship.

In a variety of ways, shifting laws and practices of the state have interacted with Marisol's subjective experiences. Her experiences have been transformed over time into technical documents in the interlinked social service and judicial systems, to be made legible to those systems in their own terms, not usually in her terms. Although Marisol emerges through this process as a gendered citizen, constituted as such largely through her performance of the feminized victim role, she refuses to be unidimensionally defined by this subject position.

"I have my independent airs," she said as we talked in 2009. "I am so conscious of what violence is, and what control is. So, now I don't accept it. Do you understand?"

Marisol's strategies to claim her rights constitute a form of resilience, and a form of agency. Her sustained engagement with me, recovering her experiences, which have been at times painful for her and at other times joyous, have to do with her deeply held conviction that social change can occur and that women should not continue living domestic violence. In the midst of one of our lengthy conversations in 2009, I told Marisol that I could send her a copy of the interview recordings. "No," she said, "You [*usted*] use it like you [*usted*] wish. Because all of this is no mystery, to me or to you. Maybe this is the least serious, and there are other women who have worse experiences. This is a way for people to see that violence exists." At that moment, I understood that her willingness to allow me to document her story is about her desire to be heard, for herself, but also as part of her self-defining mission to educate other women and impact the systems that serve women who suffer domestic violence. She envisions her engagement with me as a way for that to occur. My writing about Marisol's experiences reflects her assertion of her agency, part of her resilience, part of what keeps her alive. These words on the page have great meaning. The words shared between us create meaning for Marisol, as does her involvement in their production; these words about Marisol's narratives are about *her* agency, *her* resilience, and *her* subjectivity.

Josefina is the central focus of Chapter 4, where we continue to explore the social nature of suffering from domestic violence, particularly the class-based suffering she endured as it interacted with domestic violence and gendered inequalities. Chapter 4 further illuminates how it is these social ills, social pathologies, that need be to "cured," not individual experiences of suffering, which can be palliated but never fully "cured."

CHAPTER 4

Entanglements of Violence and Individualized "Cures"

> When I arrived into this world, they received me without any
> guarantee of love or attention. Nobody celebrated my arrival.
> I am an unwanted being, and everything announced that this
> world for me would be about abandonment, lack of affection,
> solitude, insecurity, and orphanhood. —Josefina's diary

"My Life and My Experiences, Marked by the Cruelty of My Destiny"

I met Josefina in 2003 at Family Care during the weekly group therapy sessions that I observed there for six months, the full course of the sessions. She was then around forty-seven years old and had been married for thirty-four years to a man more than a decade her senior. Josefina was always meticulously dressed, with perfectly drawn makeup and neat, manicured, blondish hair. Often, especially as a child, people had admired her complexion for being "so white." She expressed pride in her pale complexion, a phenotypic categorization often associated with social capital in Chilean society. She also talked proudly about her overall natural beauty and her aged but remarkably unwrinkled skin. She explained to me why she appeared to be younger than she was: "This is how I am naturally. I've never used any kind of cream." In addition to attending the group therapy sessions, I had the opportunity to get to know Josefina through frequent one-on-one conversations and several interviews I conducted with her in 2003. After some time, Josefina shared her diary, which she had entitled "My Life and My Experiences, Marked by the Cruelty of My Destiny," with me, an act of great trust. I interviewed her again in 2009, when she revealed a more politically oriented analysis of her suffering. From my first meeting with Josefina until the last time I talked with her in 2009, she expressed a great desire to be heard and for people to *act upon* her suffering.

Josefina's mother had abandoned her as a baby, and Josefina described her with disdain as a woman who was "illiterate" and "without feelings." Friends of the family adopted Josefina, but when she was around six years old her adoptive mother fell ill and her adoptive father began having trouble at work. From there, Josefina's memories were filled with violations. Josefina remembered that when she was seven years old an older man seduced her with candy and then raped her. She painfully recounted that she had no social networks in which to seek refuge. She was ridiculed at school for her old clothing and lack of proper materials—in essence, for her poverty. Eventually, Josefina was sent to live with an "aunt and uncle" who did away with her birth name and gave her a "new" name. "I felt a lot of pain in my soul," Josefina told me.

> Everything made me vomit. . . . All the time she made me do more work and harmed me physically. She gave me three fractures in my head and left me unconscious. She made me get up at 6 a.m. and go to bed at 11 p.m. . . . I told God I didn't want to be in this world. . . . It was impossible for me to understand why I was trapped in a pained soul, without having sinned. I always asked God to take me because it wasn't right to live without love, without affection, a childhood destroyed, that nothing could give back.

Josefina's was an arranged marriage. Her husband's brutal sexual violence against her on their wedding night was the beginning of a lifetime of suffering she spent with him.

"I bled for more than a year," she told me. "Because every time I was with him—because he was a twenty-three-year-old man, and I, twelve years old—I bled. I always bled."

Josefina soon found herself pregnant twice in rapid succession. During her first pregnancy Josefina did not receive "adequate nutrition," and her very young adolescent body "had to handle all of that."

Furthermore, she said, her scars from when she had been sexually abused as a child "never healed." She expressed how she felt:

> I suffered so much pain in my soul because I didn't have anyone. I was so sad not to have a mother, sisters and brothers, not a single family member, and without feeling loved by anyone, much less the father of my children. . . . [But] I couldn't repeat my history with [my children]. I had to deal with everything [i.e., the abuse] to be able to give them a mother and a father.

Josefina worked primarily caring for her home and children but periodically also engaged in microenterprise schemes, selling sweets and clothing items to help pay for her basic necessities. While at Family Care she worked at times with a friend selling towels they had sewn with ribbon and other adornments. Basically, however, she was financially dependent on her husband, who controlled their economic resources. My impression of Josefina's class status, based on her narratives, was that she and her husband hung on by a fraying thread to the lower edges of the lower middle class.

Josefina talked about her possibilities for recovery and recuperation in terms of economic resources:

> I have suffered rape, humiliation, being treated worse than a prostitute, something that can't be repaired. There is nothing in life that could give me back everything I have suffered. Nothing, nothing, nothing, unless someone told me, like some magic of God, "Josefina, here you have a room to live." I think that would be the most fantastic gift in the world and to be able to work to feed myself and live alone. . . . To think about myself, to be at peace with myself, to try to forget everything that has happened to me. Because if I am with the aggressor, I am with the person who has hurt me the most. It is impossible.

How does it feel to be Josefina, in this moment? Although it is impossible to inhabit her lived experience, perhaps her narrative provides a window: "Whatever he says to me is like a wound that I have from here to the middle of my body. So everything is a scratch. And that wound is open until the end. That's what he's done to me." Again in 2009, Josefina alluded to suicide, as she had often in 2003. "Sometimes when one has fought a lot it's almost like nothing's worth it. . . . My children were everything, and now I don't have any of them in my house. What motivation do I have to be there?" She continued, "It's tiring to remember these things. There are people who say that one forgets, but one cannot forget."

Josefina's account illuminates how forms of normalized and symbolic violence and structural and domestic violence were mutually constituted in her experiences within a particular historical and individual context. Her family was victim to the dictatorship's state violence and repression, another important aspect of her troubled relationship to the Chilean state. Her story shows how gendered intimate partner violence is a node or crystallization of the synergistic interactions of various forms of violence, many of which radiate outward from the state and show how the state gets "under the skin" (Molé 2011) in gendered ways. Her suffering and encounters with the state, its violence and forms of care, in many ways reflect the experiences of other women I interviewed and the social and institutional realities I observed. This chapter continues taking apart and identifying various experiences of violence, often related to the state. It shows what these entanglements of violence have done to Josefina, in her own estimation. Although Josefina's life was entangled in various forms of violence—domestic, state, symbolic, normalized, ordinary—which produced suffering in social interaction with others, the interventions she experienced were largely medicalized and individualized.

Josefina at Family Care

At Family Care Josefina attended group therapy sessions and met with a therapist in individual sessions, which meant that her situation was one of the worst that they were handling at the time. Usually women were triaged into group therapy and out of individual therapy because there was more limited space for individual sessions, which were reserved for the women "diagnosed" as being most in need. Through triage, ailments are ranked according to a designated measure of severity. In a sense, triage is a process by which institutions and their members deem a person's suffering more or less than someone else's, and thereby decide whose suffering to address first and with the most resources. At Family Care, the immediacy of women's suffering was assessed from the first instance of care, the intake, to the final outcome when women were *dado de alta* (discharged). From the first encounter, women were constantly monitored, discussed, and evaluated by individual staff members and at staff meetings, where they discussed women's cases and made decisions about whose needs were most severe and whose needs they thought they could actually address. Staff members were aware that they could not serve everyone's needs and that they needed to prioritize some women's suffering over others. Triage became a part of the "normal" functioning of this agency. Insofar as this process led to lack of care or lack of adequate care for those deemed less deserving, triage in agencies for women who suffer domestic violence can be thought of as an important form of "normalized" violence (Bourgois 2009). When Josefina was not provided adequate and timely care due to such normalized violence, the intimate gendered violence she experienced was allowed to persist.

At Family Care during 2002 and 2003 there was consistently a long waiting list of women who had made contact but who were not receiving care because the organization simply did not have the resources to care for them. A woman I knew through Safe Space told me that a friend of hers had waited a year to be seen by therapists at Family Care. I observed many instances where women needed more support than they were given, largely because staff members' hands were tied by lack of sufficient hours for interactions with clients, burnout, and lack of resources. These decisions shaped how women's fates unfolded and determined the resources they could access. The number of women Family Care could provide services for was in large part determined by the resources given to Family Care by the municipality—a bureaucratic reality that placed the sufferers further away from those who ultimately decided the allocation of government resources. Luckily for her, Josefina's situation had been deemed sufficiently severe to merit individual therapy—which entitled her to more resources from local and national governments.

Dictatorial Persecution and Symbolic Violence

During the early 1970s, Josefina explained to me, her husband worked at the Yarur textile factory in Santiago, which was a locus of workers' rights activism and socialized under Allende (see Winn 1986). During Allende's presidency, her husband had appeared on television to publicize the abuses the workers at Yarur endured, including, as Josefina said, "a miserable wage" and an arrangement of indentured servitude in which workers paid the company for room and board and were left with little money to pay for food and other necessities. Josefina said they had often gone hungry before Allende's socialist reforms. Allende's government intervened in the Yarur factory in 1971 by seizing and socializing it, turning control over to the workers. During and following the 1973 coup, the state targeted individuals and groups even tangentially related to Allende's socialist project, including workers at Yarur. Josefina explained that because of her husband's appearances on television criticizing capitalist labor abuses, the state's agents imagined him to be a leader of the workers' movement at Yarur. As a result, she told me, he was fired immediately after the coup and then "persecuted" throughout the dictatorial era by the DINA (Dirección de Inteligencia Nacional, or National Intelligence Agency). "On September 11 [1973]," Josefina told me, "They threw him out of the factory right away. They called him every [bad] name: communist, *MIRista*,[1] activist . . . simply for the interview on TV. For fourteen years, he wasn't allowed to work." By this she meant that he was not allowed to keep a job. She felt that the difficulty her husband had in finding and maintaining a job in the face of the state's repression of his opportunities magnified her lifelong class- and gender-based suffering:

> In addition to everything I had suffered, I also had to suffer the persecution of the military, and I had nothing to do with it. I had to take my four babies to eat at a parish. I had to pass by soldiers, and I went past them crying because they humiliated all of us. They stepped

on all of us. For those of us who stayed in Chile we were the most downtrodden that there could be. Without anything.

For him [her husband], it was like clipping his wings. They cut short his youth. They brought him down in every way. Because wherever he went, he was watched. And he didn't have anything.

"All the time he was working . . . just to put a can of Nescafé on the table," and then, she said, he would return home and rape her. "Before, they didn't talk about that. Before, we housewives were raped by our own husbands. I remember a day when I had a temperature of thirty-nine degrees [Celsius; 102 degrees F], and my husband had relations with me."

Now, however, discourse around violence against women is both developed and admissible. There is a language, which Josefina mobilized, to talk about the rape and abuse.

Josefina continued to explain how the DINA made it difficult for her husband to find stable work. In Josefina's analysis, she linked the DINA's pursuit of her husband to her financial woes, since her fortune was tied to his. But she also noted that this situation was intensified by the overall context of high poverty in Chile during the 1980s. She told me: "He went to work at FAMAE [Fábricas y Maestranzas del Ejército de Chile] . . . which was a military thing, where they made shells." FAMAE is a Chilean government-owned weapons factory still in operation. Josefina continued:

FAMAE was here where the new judicial courts [see Chapter 3] are now. . . . He went to work there with a brother. . . . He was working . . . and a man came in who was not a worker, dressed up as a *huaso* [cowboy]. . . . And he [the *huaso*] began to tell [tales], "Listen, they fired me from some place." The workers fell for it. He [her husband] said, "They fired me in '73. I was thrown out. They didn't wait three days." They asked [her husband] about Yarur. . . . Four military men came in pointing their guns at his back, and they told him that he had two minutes to get out of there, without any questions, without giving him any explanation or anything. Only for the fact of having worked in the factory made him a Red [i.e., communist]. . . . And that happened in all of his jobs. He would have three months in one place, one month in another.

In Josefina's narrative in 2009, she insisted that she did not sit idly by as her family suffered for her husband's supposed involvement in labor organizing during the early 1970s. She described to me, with a mixture of pride and deep frustration, how she had embodied the gender role of immaculate housewife and mother to protest the poverty in which she lived and to try to leverage help from Pinochet's government.

According to Pinochet, women were to be subordinate to men, acting as nurturing mothers, obedient wives, and immaculate house-keepers (Valdés et al 1989; see Richards 2004). In many ways the internalization of these gendered expectations emerge in Josefina's narratives. These gendered expectations, promoted and to some extent enforced by the state, created the conditions of possibility for symbolic violence to occur. Josefina talked about how she tried to fulfill these dominant expectations of women in order to claim her personhood. She internalized these expectations as truth. In her narrative to me, she used her performance of hygienic femininity to validate her claim that she deserved help from the state. She was performing her duties, as directed by the state. Now she deserved help. In this way, assumptions about the "private," domestic sphere as the appropriate domain for women to assert themselves became a naturalized and insidious form of violence. These internalized assumptions functioned to perpetuate Josefina's suffering and to reduce her ability to assert herself and have her needs met. Symbolic violence operates at a psychological level. It is one way that the state's policies and projects can get under the skin, can embed themselves in the psyche. Women's inequality and rigid gendered expectations were encoded in the state's policies, and in Josefina's narrative the state's gendered ideologies were linked with her subordination and subjugation to violence in her home.

Josefina embodied these naturalized gender roles in order to prove that she was a person of value within the society and therefore a person who deserved help. Josefina described her enactment of gender roles that equate cleanliness with feminine value as simply "the way things are."

"I thought that basically I was born simply so that I could be a mother. Not a woman, with a name," she told me.

Here, structural and domestic violence interacted with symbolic violence. Once at Family Care, Josefina could begin to name such a thought process as a form of suffering imposed by others and thereby challenge some of the gendered expectations that constituted symbolic violence for her.

Josefina's mobilization of dominant feminine gender roles is part of a broader pattern of women's mobilization of feminine moralities to claim power and authority. In her analysis of women's movements in Chile, Power (2002) illuminates how the right-wing women's movement in the 1970s, Poder Femenino (Feminine Power), rallied against Allende's government, drawing moral authority from their essentialized feminine roles as mothers, the biological and social reproducers of the nation. In a similar fashion, Josefina mobilized her moral authority as a mother in order to protest her class-based captivity during the dictatorship era. She told me about a letter she wrote to Santiago Mayor Carlos Bombal, a Pinochet appointee (1981–1987). Josefina described the mayor's response:

Señora Bombal [the mayor's wife] came to my house. . . . She thought she would see a dirty woman, with the children's noses running. Because here in Chile, unfortunately, poverty is associated with filth. And I am different. Because I can have two boxes to sit on, but if I can, I polish those boxes everyday with a gift-wrap paper so that they look better. I am not going to hide that which I cannot hide. Poverty is impossible, and I can't [hide it] because it's something that is part of me. They taught me that the house has to be clean . . . when you are expecting a visitor. They taught me that when I was a little girl, and for me that's how it is. . . . They came to offer me I think three hundred pesos. . . . So I told her [the mayor's wife] that she should put herself in my place for a moment. "How would you like it if, with that money [300 pesos], you had to pay electricity, buy gas, buy milk for the children, fruit, health care. *My children are my children. They are not animals.* They are children, whom I have to prepare for the future. They are men. I have three men. . . . Here you are not going to find an old woman without teeth, filthy," I told her, "and children with lice, nor with their noses running. Because for me that isn't [caused by] poverty. That for me is people who don't want to get ahead and who send out their children to beg, and I don't do that. I sent a letter so that you could judge for yourself." She did not even want to come in because my floor [was gleaming]. I shined it all the time. Everything was clean, and that's what she arrived to see. She saw that there was no necessity. There was no poverty. There was no lack of food. I told her, "Look at my fridge. Look at what I have. I don't have anything in this moment to feed my children." She didn't even want to come in to see. Because she was at the entrance of the house and saw that it was impeccably clean.

In response to Josefina's efforts and embodiment of an immaculate, hygienic femininity, which she felt would give her the moral authority to successfully protest her situation, the municipality offered her a coupon to receive free food at a camp nearby. "And I went there," Josefina told me, "which I really regretted, because they offered me corn." She expressed anger and disbelief at what she felt was the government's inadequate and degrading response to her needs.

> Corn? But I don't have chickens. I have children. I thought that they were going to help me, [with] milk, sugar, the basics. When one is badly off, milk, sugar, a little oil, rice, pasta, is enough, but they gave me corn, wheat berries, and some bottom-of-the-barrel tea leaves. I wasn't going to accept that because instead of lifting up the poor person, they humiliate her. They denigrate her.

Josefina described how she had engaged in various other activities to attempt to ameliorate her family's position of class-based subordination during the dictatorship. She remembered fondly when she worked at the Vicaría de Solidaridad (Vicariate of Solidarity), run by the Catholic Church (see Agosín 2007). She said with pride:

> The Vicaría never simply gave to us. They taught us, with dignity, how to earn our money, making weavings, knitting bags, which seemed horrible to us. But the foreigners bought them because they knew the

persecution that was going on in Chile. So we didn't feel denigrated, as though they were just giving to us. We felt that we were working, and sending things out of the country.

She described putting her children to bed and then working until 4 a.m. After sleeping for two hours, she was up again to take her children to school and make bread to sell.

"I have a lot to tell, in truth," Josefina reflected at this point in our conversation in 2009. I had heard none of these facets of her life experience during the time I spent listening to her narrative in 2003, whether in our individual interviews, my conversations with her, or in group therapy sessions. Josefina's opening up in new ways over the years demonstrates the value of long-term ethnographic engagement with women who have suffered domestic violence for understanding the ways that their narratives and experiences shift over time.

La Alegría Nunca Llegó (The Joy Never Came)

At one point in our conversation in 2009, Josefina looked at me with disappointment and anger in her voice and declared, "La alegría nunca llegó" (The joy never came), a reworking of the antidictatorship slogan of the late 1980s, "La Alegría Ya Viene" (The Joy Is Coming). By 2009, Josefina's narrative reflected an overall ethos of dissatisfaction with the Concertación among Chileans. The Concertación is the center-left political coalition that won the first postdictatorship democratic presidential election and held the presidency until 2010. The Concertación had been elected to replace Pinochet in part on their promise to reverse the dictatorship's repressive policies and practices and bring social justice, true democracy, and democratic prosperity to all Chilean people. By the last few years of the Concertación's tenure, Chileans' dissatisfaction with its failure to produce the promised results was palpable, as many felt that promises made for democracy and equality during the postdictatorship era had not been fulfilled. Disillusionment reigned as neoliberal structures and projects, along with the attendant chasms between rich and poor, became increasingly entrenched. I was surprised by this shift in Josefina's narrative of her suffering. In her narrative rendition of her life in 2009, Josefina wove together her critique of the Concertación with her vehement rejection of the class-based dictatorial violence undergone by her husband and therefore her family and of the specifically gendered and intimate suffering she endured.

In advertisements in the lead-up to the official transition from the dictatorial regime to a democratic government in 1990, the Concertación's slogan "La Alegría Ya Viene" was ubiquitous. Hopes ran high in that period. Paley (2001) described the Concertación's promises for a newly democratic era during their campaign: "[an] image of poverty shown in [a] television commercial was accompanied by a hopeful message: voting Pinochet out of office could bring an end to hunger and misery. Whereas poverty was attributed to dictatorship, democracy was associated with economic betterment."

By reformulating that claim, which had once signified liberation and the promise of democracy and equality, Josefina expressed a resounding critique of the postdictatorship Chilean state, which had failed to fulfill the promise of equality and a better life for those at the bottom. By 2009, Josefina's hopes for happiness and economic opportunity had been dashed. Neoliberal democracy had utterly failed her. She told me that she would like to be able to say:

> The government, the municipality, did something for me. They loved me as a Chilean woman, as the person that I am. That, for me, would be the most beautiful thing that could happen. . . . Not just any person gets married at twelve years old. I suffered changes to my name. I suffered rape when I was seven. I deal with an idiotic man up until the present day, who doesn't even give me money to buy deodorant.

"It's true that money helps a lot," she said, "but the material is the material. Really it is us as people that have value. But now we are more into the material than the personal, unfortunately." Josefina continued in her analysis of the long-term repercussions of the dictatorial policies:

> They did all of this that affects the third generation, our children, our grandchildren. Because just like the children had a bad time, the children can't give now a beautiful childhood [to their children]. . . .

My God, what were those people [authors of the dictatorial policies]
thinking? With what conscience are they going to die? We are human
beings.

Once again, Josefina launched an incisive critique of class inequality—
related to her own and especially her children's and grandchildren's
well-being. She told me emphatically:

> *There is no solution. It is us poor people who are going to suffer.* [For
> example] there is the underground highway direct to the airport for
> the rich. . . . They don't go on public transportation. None of the
> politicians ride TranSantiago [the public transportation system, widely
> regarded as a failure of public policy]. From the Plaza [Plaza Italia, in
> the middle of downtown] up, it's another world [indicating the upper-
> middle-class and upper-class neighborhoods of Santiago]. And down
> below it's the worst. Unfortunately, the ones on the bottom want to
> give their wealth to those at the top. Those at the bottom are the ones
> who work, the workers, the ones who do everything.
>
> The damage that has been done to the workers hasn't been
> repaired. My husband goes to a meeting [of survivors of the
> dictatorship's violence] where the exonerated people get together,
> where you see people who were tortured . . . with the neck broken,
> spine broken. They raped pregnant women, and they lost those
> children . . . I saw it. I see these people suffering who are still waiting
> for the president [Bachelet] to pay them. And still they go out to the
> street and get shot with water [with dictatorship-era water cannons], so
> that they can't protest.

During the postdictatorship period, Josefina's husband was designated
as a victim of the dictatorship and was exonerated, and for that he re-
ceives a monthly stipend from the government. Josefina is glad for
the financial support, but she remains confused by the term "exonerated" because she feels it does not apply to her husband because he
was "never a communist, never was political, never anything." Josefina
told me that he explained to her that "we were survivors of the dictatorship without having had anything to do with it." Here she reminded

me that at the time of the coup, when her husband was blacklisted by Pinochet's regime, she was fifteen years old, married and with two children. Although she was also clearly a victim of the dictatorship, he— not she—is the one who is paid for their mutual suffering. Neither her house nor her income is in her own name. Both she and her husband can receive treatment at the Chilean government's Program for Reparations and Integrated Support in Health and Rights (Programa de Reparación y Ayuda Integral en Salud y Derechos, or PRAIS) because they are "exonerated." But, she said, "Often the public services do not even have aspirin. . . . In the hospitals the patients are in the hallways. There is not good medical treatment."

"There has never been democracy. The joy never came," she said emphatically. "Here we have never had justice, nor joy, nor democracy."[2]

Gendered Structural Violence and Economic Domestic Violence

For many women like Josefina, class-based inequalities and struggles intersect with gendered economic inequalities. This intersection has historically been entrenched in the wider society *and* in women's intimate relationships. Of the eighteen women who shared their life histories with me, I estimate that all but one, whose family seemed to have been middle class, were lower middle class to lower class. Here I refer to the economic situations of families; often women were in more negative economic situations than their abusive partners because of the various interlocking forms of abuse and inequalities they suffered. Ten women spontaneously reported that they had experienced economic domestic violence. Half of those I interviewed were engaged in some kind of remunerative work, while the other half were strictly homemakers. Formal wage labor included managing a hospital cafeteria, managing a picture-framing business, and working as an administrative assistant. Several women sold small handicrafts—towels with lace trim, candies, and clothing. This kind of low-paying, unstable, and under-the-table income generation, while not enough for subsistence, reflected women's agency.

Josefina's strong desire to leave her husband was overshadowed by a strong ambivalence connected to her lack of viable options for supporting herself economically. Josefina often said she would take a job as a live-in nanny; however, when such "opportunities" arose, she did not take them. She was conflicted about leaving her home because she would have to abandon everything: most of her material possessions; her comfort, albeit a cold sort of comfort; and the place where she had raised her children. She would have to leave all of this not for "a room to live . . . alone . . . to be at peace," which was her expressed desire, but for a small room in someone else's house where she would have been both full-time maid and childcare provider (usually six days a week, with near-constant availability), with a salary of about US$160 per month, too little to afford her own place.

Josefina was at Family Care in 2003, before the passage of the divorce law. Even after divorce became legal in 2004, it did not provide a viable way out for her. Josefina would have lost financially in a divorce because she would not have had access to her husband's pension or his benefits as an "exonerated" victim of the dictatorship's violence. Her real options for changing the structural conditions of her life were very limited. If she moved out of her home without a divorce, she would have had to fend for herself, sacrificing one safety in order to get another (see Adelman 2004). Josefina's situation underlines how the dearth of opportunities, due largely to economic restrictions, not only helps to perpetuate intimate experiences of abuse but is an integral part of the abuse. From a perspective that individualizes blame, Josefina's "failure" to take a job as a nanny constituted "missed opportunities" to provide for herself. From Josefina's perspective, the "opportunities" that arose for her presented neither real options to improve her life nor possibilities to escape into something better.

In our conversation in 2009, Josefina's narrative of captivity and suffering still contained elements of her economic dependence on her husband and her lack of work opportunities in the wider society. She explained to me how her husband used his ownership of their home as a form of abuse and control. He was able to do so because he was the worker who had made the money to pay the 5 percent down payment for the house. Sometimes, Josefina told me, he would say, "Well, if you are annoyed with me, why don't you move? You go. The house is mine."

"So, I was always quiet for the children, to avoid making problems for the children. I dealt with it up to the present day. . . . He controls me. He doesn't give me money," Josefina said.

The onus was on Josefina to actively and persistently seek help for herself. Services available for her largely focused on therapeutic interventions that did not address her fundamental needs—work, shelter, food, and economic stability for the future. In these ways, programs for domestic violence, such as Family Care's, while helpful, sometimes also inadvertently entrench what some scholars have identified as the neoliberal ideals of self-efficacy and individual responsibility. Merry (2001:19) has theorized that a "transnational movement toward self-management and neoliberal governance" underlies a new emphasis on psychotherapy as a mechanism for internalized social control (cf. Goldstein 2004:30).[3] I observed how this individualizing of women's responsibilities for escaping their violent relationships manifested in Family Care's practices.

For example, at one of their weekly staff meetings, one of the therapists initiated a discussion about her frustration with Josefina's lack of initiative to move out of her house and make the changes in her life that she talked about over and over, week after week, month after month. Another staff member responded to this concern with the hypothesis that Josefina needed more time to reflect and make a connection with the therapist, pointing out that work with women who suffer domestic violence is necessarily based on long-term goals. Another therapist advocated that they must not distance themselves from Josefina, yet at the same time should "give her wings" and space to make her own decisions. Another suggested delving into Josefina's family life and analyzing how she related to authority as a youth, to understand the roots of her behaviors. Someone else emphasized that decisions should be left up to the individual woman; therapists should help her develop tools to recover, but should recognize that progress is often varied and disorganized. It is difficult to know when or how changes will occur in a person, she pointed out, but with time, hopefully the patient will realize her possibilities.

This kind of individualizing ethic went against what I knew of Josefina. She had clearly explained during group therapy sessions and to me in our individual interviews that her not leaving was directly tied to her very real lack of economic possibilities should she choose to leave the relationship. Developing coping skills or interior psychological self-talk and self-esteem by itself would not allow her to "spread her wings." She felt she needed viable economic opportunities in order to escape the abuse. While she expressed that she valued the psychologically oriented work she was engaged in at Family Care, she felt that this alone was not enough to make possible the changes she wished for in her life. She needed material supports that were simply not available.

Social Pains: Individualizing Therapies

Psychiatric treatments also served to individualize Josefina's suffering. In 2003, she talked about the psychoactive medications she took, including antidepressants and lithium, and, in 2009, she continued to be pharmaceutically maintained (Biehl 2005). She had recently been taking alprazolam (Xanax) for depression and clonazepam (Klonopin) for anxiety. She took an expensive sleeping pill instead of these older-generation drugs when she could afford it or could obtain free samples (see also Das and Das 2007). She preferred this sleep medication because it did not make her feel "high" like the alprazolam and clonazepam. Her government health plan covered alprazolam and clonazepam, which she believed were highly addictive, but did not cover the more expensive sleeping pill, with its relative lack of negative side effects. When pharmaceuticals are off-patent they are vastly cheaper to consume, which is why government health plans often cover older-generation drugs whose efficacy can be less and whose side effects are often greater than newer drugs. Josefina's recovery was beholden to market forces. The drugs that were to maintain her alive, if not thriving, were not top quality; she knew this but could rarely do anything about it. She regularly had to take the older medications and suffer their iatrogenic effects. The day of our interview in 2009, she told me that she had just run out of the expensive sleep medicine, although her physician had given her free samples to tide her over.

"I don't sleep even though I drink the healing waters," she told me, alluding to a form of self-medication within her reach that she presumably used when she did not have the expensive pharmaceutical.

She added that she might have had the money to pay for the expensive medication if her son, who has three children and no stable job, had not recently had to have his wisdom teeth removed, which she and her husband funded. His lack of a stable job and health problems presented another economic and emotional burden for Josefina, and this prevented her from accessing the best care for herself. "He was born in the thick of the dictatorship," Josefina explained. "They never let him do his military service because he was the son of a 'communist.' My son doesn't even have that."

Josefina lamented that because she had no money, she was also forced to go to the underfunded public health clinics to get treatment and medications. Each month, Josefina dutifully got up early, applied her makeup, dressed herself up, and struggled to find transportation to make it to the clinic on time, where she then waited in line for hours to receive lower-quality medications.

Josefina's first challenge to receive her medications each month was her lack of money for transportation to get to the clinic. She had to depend on her husband or son to transport her because she disdained the public transportation system, TranSantiago, put in place under the administration of Concertación President Ricardo Lagos. Again the poor lost, she felt: "It's a lot worse. The *micros* [buses] are uncomfortable, and taking the metro is just too much. . . . For me it's humiliating. I mean, beyond having all of these problems, one has to deal with that. . . . In the used buses they brought, you feel every bump."

Again, Josefina's disappointment with the Concertación's promise that "joy is coming" for all Chileans was palpable. Her disillusionment was crystallized in the failure of TranSantiago to provide dignified and affordable transportation for those forced to use it. Josefina said bitterly: "I hate Pinochet and Lagos both. Because Lagos was the one who presented the famous [Tran]Santiago. And he was the one who pointed his finger at that man [Pinochet] and said that they were going to do justice. He's [Lagos] a traitor and a dog." Sometimes, Josefina arrived at the clinic on foot because the transportation provided by TranSantiago was so expensive and inefficient. "I have even arrived crying because my feet were totally worn out," she complained.

Once at the clinic to receive her monthly doses, "It's all bureaucracy, and it's horrible," Josefina lamented. She did not accept her subjugation to dehumanizing treatment without critique. "It makes the poor people feel more denigrated." She explained:

> The lack is notable. There are three nurses who don't come anymore. My psychologist got sick, so it's not like we're seeing a fluid rhythm. There are a lot of firings. You're seeing, "Don't come. The doctor isn't coming." So you get depressed. . . . Why aren't the clinics nicer? It's an old house. It's not painted. So, it's not nice for the people who have to work there. They are not very happy. If a person isn't well paid, or they aren't happy, then they're not going to give a good service, either.
>
> When I go for them to give me my medications, so the psychiatrist can give them to me, I have to wait in line for two hours. I go at six in the morning, and from there I leave at two something in the afternoon, many times without breakfast or lunch. You have to be waiting all day, and one sees everything. So, basically, we get sicker. It makes us sicker to see all of that, to see so many people with the same sickness, and I am very suspicious in that way. . . . The service of the hospitals is really bad.

"If one arrives sick, it makes them feel worse," she emphasized. She wishes instead for a caring system where they would say to her, "'*M'ijita*, here. Take. Here is the prescription.' That would be so lovely." (*M'ijita* is a contracted form of *mi hijita*, which is translated literally as "my little daughter" and figuratively as "sweetie." This term can have a condescending connotation when said to a woman.)

Josefina felt that although she persisted in seeking help, she continued to suffer humiliation, frustration, and depression from the institutions that were supposed to provide care. Again, she wished for both material and affective resources. Instead, she received individualized and ongoing psychiatric forms of care, dispensed in what she felt was a dehumanizing way.

Conclusion

Various forms of normalized, structural, state, and symbolic violence acted to constrain Josefina within the confines of her abusive relationship with her husband. Her narratives demonstrate how these various forms of violence are *part of* domestic violence and its attendant suffering. Josefina's entanglement within various forms of violence is part of a wider pattern of socially produced suffering that women experience disproportionately to men—in Chile, in the United States, and throughout the world. Her processes of recovery were complicated most pointedly by an ongoing relationship with her abusive husband—a relationship largely based on her economic dependence on him. This kind of economic dependence is a widespread reality for women because many stay home to raise their children instead of working for wages and accruing a pension. Josefina's processes of help-seeking, recovery, and transformation were fragmented because of this ongoing dependence and for other reasons as well, including her "entire lifetime of suffering." Thus, the idea of a linear progression toward a fixed goal labeled "recovery" does not fit with Josefina's experiences. Clinging to a linear concept geared toward the end point of complete recovery can frustrate efforts to provide adequate care.

Yet the treatments Josefina could access from the state were almost exclusively individualized and often psychopharmacological, acting only at the level of bare biology. The medications were free and, although they may have had some positive effects, Josefina found the social experiences surrounding their procurement demoralizing and degrading. She sensed that she was not receiving the layers of care that she needed, which would have had to extend beyond the level of addressing her biochemical makeup through psychopharmacological interventions.

Josefina had clear ideas about what she needed in order to escape her abusive marriage and recover to some extent, and she lamented that the kinds of services and resources she felt she needed were not available. She wished for the state's material support in the form of housing away from her husband and for computer-skills training that she imagined would allow her to find the kind of dignified and well-paid-enough work she envisioned for herself. She wished also for the intangible and affective. Josefina told me that she longed for time and space.

> To get to know oneself, two months at least, to know how one is, to do sort of an interior exam, to think. Because I have suffered so much. . . . I wish they would treat me with joy. [I wish] I would find people with a helping spirit, to make life more enjoyable, so that I could have affection for life. . . . In my case I have tried [to kill myself] five times, because I couldn't handle it anymore.

She also wished for "a center where we [women] could be, where we could share our pain, and also our joy." "Health has to be first," she told me.

Although entanglements of violence are entrenched and recovery is perhaps never complete, forms of *sanación*, or healing, as Luz called her processes, explored in Chapter 5, are possible.

CHAPTER 5

Sanación

Excavating the "Ordinary"
to Move beyond Violence and Misery

Individual lives are defined by context, but they are also
generative of new contexts. —Veena Das (2000:210)

"My history has many marks of violence," Luz told me in 2009 as we
sat at a busy Santiago restaurant, an audio recorder between us on the
table.[1]

> One type of violence that I suffered was when I was in my mother's
> belly, and my mother wanted to have a son. She didn't want to
> have a daughter. . . . That is very difficult [*fuerte*]. . . . She had an
> unwanted pregnancy. For my father to accept it, she wanted to have
> a son, a man, because she already had a daughter. . . . And she waits
> the nine months, and I am born. . . . I think that was a very difficult
> moment. . . . That marks the history of a person. You realize, if you
> start to look, that there is an entire lifetime [of violence], which I think
> is the life of all women, in one way or another.

Soon after telling me this Luz said, "In this process of *sanación* [heal-
ing], I have been discovering things that are sadder." She remembered
having experienced sexual abuse as a child, another instance in which
her intimate, family sphere—where the most primary affective ties are
supposed to be forged—was the place where she underwent violence.
Because she felt estranged from her mother, which she attributes to
her mother's rejection of her for being female, she felt she had no one
to tell about the abuse. She also suffered because she was lesbian and

felt she had to keep her sexuality secret. "There, too, is damage," she noted.

Ema introduced Luz to me less than a year after Luz's husband had attempted to murder her and then killed himself. We met on a sunny late summer afternoon in 2003 at the Women's Place, a grassroots organization close to Safe Space, in the midst of a fundraising event to support a group of young women in their travels to a World Social Forum meeting in Brazil. The Women's Place was bubbling with activity, including Ema's tarot card readings, which were especially popular, and yoga. Following that first encounter, Luz and I had various conversations in 2003 and 2004, and again in 2009, when she shared her suffering and processes of *sanación* with me.

At one point in our conversations in 2009, I asked Luz if she would like me to use her name or a pseudonym in my writing about her life. She asked me to use a pseudonym, but not something *gringa*, she said with a smile. Then she answered the question in a more profound way, to tell me why she was participating in this project:

> I know you. That's a factor. There is volition to your work. I value
> your work. It's very important, what you do. And also, there's the trust
> already, and I'm realizing that it's good for me too, to talk about it
> with you, because you have a different perspective. It has meaning.
> It has another meaning, and I think that also permits me to realize
> everything that happened, to review a little. It's like looking back, to
> see the differences. It's very positive. . . . You know, when you wrote
> me the e-mail [sent before my visit in 2009 to ask her if we could
> meet], I was impressed, because it was an opportune time. Maybe if
> it had been a different moment, I wouldn't have given the time. But,
> you arrived in a special moment for me. Because I have permitted
> myself to remember things, facts, to look back and take the value from
> that, not only staying in the pain and in the negative, but also to [draw
> from] the very positive things.

"How does it feel to talk with me about all of this now?" I asked Luz.

"It's been a long time since I've talked about this problem," she told me, "because before it was very painful for me. But now my recovery of the strength, the desire, the value, gives me strength for other things. I can use that energy, that strength, for positive things."

Later in the conversation, she revealed another reason for her participation in the cocreation of her narrative with me as interpreter:

> Here, they have marches against femicide, and you know what
> they do? Some women from the organizations, they go and paint
> themselves with fake bruises and put on bandages. I don't think that's
> the way to do it. Why don't they show histories of women who have
> overcome the life of violence, and who have brought their children
> up, and have been able to work, and have achieved a regular life,
> without the necessity of staying with an abusive man?

Luz's Life History Narrative

Luz's early life in her family of origin was marked by state violence and the predominance of gendered ideals based in women's inequality. During her adolescent years, her family was active in the class-based struggles of Allende's Unidad Popular. Luz's father had been a Communist Party member, blacklisted by the government during the 1950s because of his involvement with unionizing mine workers. His restaurant in Santiago was a meeting place for left-wing activists, and Luz remembers that President Salvador Allende, who died in the 1973 coup, had been there once for a meeting. She remembered that period of her life fondly. Her father's activism for class equality, she noted, did not translate into commensurate attitudes about gender equality. Luz wanted to study to be an electronic technician, but he felt that career "was not for women." He placed her in a school for girls where she could study gender "appropriate" subjects. She continued:

> My father wasn't a man who hit, or anything like that. . . . There
> wasn't the issue of physical violence, or anything, but yes, in his
> relationship with her [Luz's mother], he was abusive. Because he
> controlled the money. He thought she didn't know how to manage the
> money. I remember that he told her that she didn't understand. *He*

didn't let her develop herself as a person. He always saw her as a weaker person. . . . That's also abuse. (emphasis added)

Luz, like Marisol, reflected on the ways domestic violence stunts personhood. Marisol had told me how constant abuse "affects one's health because, psychologically, one sees that one is affected because one realizes that she can't develop herself as a person."

Luz's analysis here, looking back on her family life, allowed her to make a statement about broader cultural patterns that she observed— within a discourse that was similar to that of the feminist movement and in particular to that of Safe Space, where she had sought care. The critique of culturally embedded gender roles that produce suffering for women in intimate relationships is strong within women's rights sectors in Chile. Luz mobilized these new frameworks in her effort to construct her life and identity *against* dominant gender roles.

From Luz's perspective, the state had failed to provide her protection from violence and therefore had denied her full citizenship, both during and after the dictatorial regime. The years of the dictatorship were filled with violence and fear for her. She recalled those years as having been "a very difficult period when you were incapacitated by everything and totally terrified. . . . [Such an experience] changes your life." Luz described the ethos:

> There was a whole machinery of fear, because of the helicopters
> that were around all day, every night, over the *población*. They are
> for combative relations. Do you understand? Santiago was divided
> up. There are sectors where leaders of the *poblaciones* organized
> [resistance], and there, they went back and forth day and night.
> Day and night. I even remember the sound of the helicopters. They
> descended, and at night shined their lights. You know there was a
> curfew? And those helicopters went all through the streets and turned
> on their lights . . . for ten or fifteen years. That's not [just] a few [years].
> Moreover, there were certain groups of soldiers who stayed in these
> *poblaciones* to protect, well, "protect" the *población*. There was an
> electricity substation, and they were guarding that from "terrorists."

They were not really "protecting" the *población*. They were protecting [the electrical substation]. They had real power over the *población* because you always saw soldiers with submachine guns, and they practiced shooting day and night. You always heard the sound of the bullets. Bullets, bullets, always.

She was not able to study at the university as she had wanted because her father's business went bankrupt and the government ceased offering financial support for university study as it had during Allende's Unidad Popular, when "a right to education" was strongly idealized.

Luz told me, "after everything that happened it was as if no one dared to even go out." She also endured violent ruptures in her social networks in the years following the coup: "I lost my circle of friends. . . . My *compañeros* [comrades/friends], almost all of them were exiled. Others were disappeared; others [were taken] prisoner."

In this context, her sister had continued to be heavily involved in the antidictatorial movement, as was Luz though to a lesser degree, and in the mid-1970s her sister was under threat of being arrested. Because of the threat of imminent arrest, her sister was granted political asylum in Canada, where her mother and some of Luz's other brothers and sisters and their children were allowed to join her. For Luz this "had a great impact . . . because for us the feeling of a big group, a big family, was very important." In 2009, Luz explained to me that she had been left behind because she was twenty years old at the time and a woman. The Canadian government took her brother, who was nineteen years old because "he was a man and he represented a support for her [sister] and the family. And me, as a woman, I was twenty. I couldn't go because I was an adult, and I didn't represent any possibility of generating income."

Left without her networks of friends and family as a result of the dictatorship's violence, Luz married and gave birth to her own children, in part to fill this void and in part to fulfill the dominant gender role of motherhood in order to repress her homosexuality. She told me, "I was fulfilling a role. I wasn't living."

"I ended up converting myself into his mother," Luz explained, speaking about her husband. "He was like another son for me." Several women confirmed this in a group interview at Family Care in 2003. This aspect of Luz and her husband's relationship existed in juxtaposition to him being, she told me, "a very *machista* man who was the boss of the situation, and he gave orders. He always told me, 'Look, I am the one who gives the orders. . . . I am the one who says if we are going to eat [at a certain hour] or not.'"

Luz's mother-in-law consistently intervened on behalf of her son's right to male dominance. Luz told me:

> My mother-in-law came to visit us on Sundays, and she told me to serve him first. You have to serve him. . . . She told me that he deserved the best. He is the boss of the house [*dueño de casa*], the man who brings in the money. And then, whenever I had an opinion, she told me, "Shut your mouth, don't talk," that I shouldn't talk or give an opinion.

Luz's mother-in-law upheld the dominant gender role of men as providers and as authoritarian heads of households. Women were supposed to work in the home, not in the wider world of remunerated labor. As Luz explained,

> There was no work that was worth it. Because, I could work as *una nana* [a nanny/maid], as a domestic servant. . . . I remember once I worked in a leather factory. I was [there] like one week. They fired me because . . . it was complicated for them to have women. They couldn't have [women] because they had to have the conditions for women, women's bathrooms and everything.

At other times, Luz knitted and sold sheets and other small items, but she said she was not very interested in money. Her husband worked and paid the bills. She told me that for him money and things were much more important than they were for her. She said, "When he made more money, he felt that he was worth more." This difference between them, she thinks, might have been because her husband grew up very poor, in rural southern Chile, whereas she grew up in Santiago and her family history is rooted in the struggle for social justice. Her grandfather had migrated from southern Peru to Santiago in search of a better life and education for his children. Her grandmother, during the Great Depression, gave everyone food. "She had a food business, and she ended up giving away half of the food and selling the other half. That's a history that is very valued in the family."

Her mother-in-law's rigid upholding of gendered ideologies was not only directed at Luz. Luz remembered: "When my daughter started university, she asked her, 'But why are you going to study? You should get married.' And we're talking about the year 2000. . . . It's very cultural. It's very deep. *To change this you have to fight constantly*" (emphasis added).

Luz referred here to her own "constant fight" to create a new social order, one not based on gendered hierarchies within family and social systems, and her constant fight to reclaim and maintain her personhood as part of this new social order. "I have a trajectory of rebellion against the system," Luz reminded me.

Searching for Care in Medical and Juridical Systems

Luz was active in seeking help for the general malaise she suffered, prior to and following the state's new focus on domestic violence.

> I went to a lot of places, you see, to ask for help. I went to a lot of places, and they always talked to me about how I had to worry about my family, how important my family was for me, my children, that I had to be happier. But they didn't ask me why I wasn't happy.

Luz described the painful effects of the "treatments" the physicians offered her, in addition to their advice about her fulfillment of gender roles.

> They gave me pills to relax, other pills to sleep. . . . It is terrible, this medication thing. Because I feel that it was a way for me not to suffer, not to *feel*. . . . [My husband] would leave on a Friday and return on Monday, and I had no problem [with it] because with my pills, I felt great.

Luz also took pills for her various aches and pains, which her doctors attributed to stress, including headaches, upset stomach, irritable colon, backaches, and shoulder aches.[2] Though she had good health care through her husband's job, none of the various specialists she saw ever asked her what might have been causing such severe stress and stress reactions; they generally individualized her problems and attributed them, as she expressed it, to "[my] character, my way of being . . . that I didn't trust, that I didn't give myself to relationships." In another instance, a doctor told her she was just experiencing premenstrual syndrome, and another suggested that she go out and buy herself something pretty in order to feel better. Luz's distress here was linked to gendered expectations promoted by powerful professionals. Her interactions with health care providers, who embodied the authoritative knowledge of biomedicine and the power to define "truth" that often accompanies such knowledge, were key instances in which gendered expectations of the self were made manifest and contributed to her entrapment (cf. Sargent and Bascope 1996).

Luz fruitlessly sought help in the judicial system on three separate occasions before her husband shot and almost killed her. Each time, the memories of the state violence of the dictatorship and what it had done to her friends and family made her fearful and hesitant to seek help from the state. She, like some of the other women I interviewed, saw danger, not safety, in the police. Luz first went to the police in the 1990s, defying her fear of the state's violence.

Luz described to me how she felt afraid, very embarrassed, and shameful when she first reported the abuse to the police. The police station felt very threatening and sinister to her, and the police seemed incompetent and uncaring. Nothing came of that first complaint, except embarrassment and shame. Luz filed her second complaint in the emergency room, after her husband had bloodied her eye.

> I waited hours for them to attend to me, and they never saw me. The doctor never saw me. . . . Imagine . . . an emergency room that is full of people, where everyone could see me, where I had . . . to tell the policeman, standing there, not in a room or anything. . . .

Then to wait for hours and not have anyone treat me. No one took care of my eye. I left. I never went back.

In 2001, Luz went to the police for the third time to request a restraining order because she feared that her husband was going to kill her. This time, she went to the Family Police Station in downtown Santiago, a police station specifically dedicated to issues of family violence, to file the complaint and request a restraining order.

I knew something about it [the Family Police Station]. I find it. I called. I asked and I made sure. I went downtown. I walked. I didn't know where to enter because the police stations are very protected places. They are afraid they will be attacked. "And you, Señora, what do you want? You, why did you come?" they said. "I came to file a complaint." The guy, kind of militaristic, speaks to you in a [rough] tone, "Go sit over there." He is going to call the police officer who is on duty. . . . Very authoritarian. There should be places to file complaints, where there is another system, not so authoritarian, when you are a victim.

Luz was visibly irritated when she talked about the various levels of incompetence in the system, which she felt ultimately contributed to her close brush with death at her husband's hands.

"They always have that kind of problem, incompetence," she said.

I don't know if they do it so you'll give up. . . . [Maybe] they do everything so that you get tired and you get bored, like one or two hours waiting . . . a terrible incompetence. . . . And I have to ask them to write things down. . . . He [the police officer] decides what he wants to write and what he doesn't want to write. . . . And I *had* the information about how to file a complaint, and what I could demand, and [still] I was only able to do it halfway well.

Even with all of the information that she had, she was only "able to do it halfway well." In response to her complaint, she received a letter saying that she needed to ratify it before they could issue a restraining order. Luz told me about what happened when she went to the court to ratify her complaint:

> I go and a woman attends to me, a court clerk. . . . And this woman looks at me and she tells me that she is very busy with a lot of work, and that I must wait for her . . . and [asks me] if I am very sure of what I am about to do. I feel that she wants to convince me otherwise. I get very annoyed. . . . And I wait. . . . [She asks me] if I am sure of what I am doing. [And tells me] that I have to be very sure, that these things are difficult. . . . I insist on the restraining order, and she tells me, "No, that isn't the right thing." Because there was no threat, nor a physical aggression where he tried to kill me. He didn't intend to kill me. It was only my "supposition." I needed to have *proof* that he wanted to kill me. I *think* that *one* of the pieces of *proof* was the *finger marks* on my throat. *I don't know* [she said with irony in her voice].

Although she presented documentation of her injuries, they were deemed to be minimal (*menos graves*) by health officials and thus they did not "count" for anything according to the judicial system. The court clerk informed her that only with "serious" injuries would they issue a restraining order.

Finally, the court issued Luz's restraining order. It was sent to her home, but she never received it because when it finally arrived, she was recuperating in the hospital after her husband attempted to murder her and then killed himself. The judicial system's incompetence had almost killed Luz. She reflected on her situation: "I think if I had been in a different emotional state, or someone among those who surrounded me. . . . We should have sued over this situation. We should have sued this official because she did not take the correct measures. . . . That would have made her publically responsible." Her comments critique a lack of accountability on the part of public officials, and constitute a powerful critique of impunity.

In juxtaposition to the judicial system's lack of attention to her suffering prior to her husband's attempt on her life, there was a drawn-out investigation around her husband's death in which Luz was heavily embroiled following her release from the hospital. She explained what happened: "They interrogated me, the court clerk, the detective. I was interrogated for many hours. I wanted them to leave. Very complicated. [They asked me] how it was that no one had helped me from inside of the house to get out." Throughout the interrogations, she had the support of Safe Space and one psychologist there, in particular, who accompanied her to the interrogations.

"I was furious with the world, that they interrogated me, that they questioned what I said. They asked me again and again," Luz told me, noting too that there had been one detective who was apologetic for putting her through all of this questioning.

"But still, I had to go through the process," she said.

They also questioned her children and her husband's family. Luz pointed out that, ironically, the court was very attentive to this part of the process, while it had failed miserably in providing a timely restraining order. Could it be, Luz implied, that a dead man was worth more somehow than a woman who was suffering? "When I talk about these things, I see their gravity," she told me.

For Luz, as for many of the women I interviewed, the arms of the state, in the form of the judicial system, had failed to protect her (Parson 2005). First, the officials of the state had treated Luz poorly, dissuading her from lodging a complaint. Then, due to time lags, Luz was almost murdered by her husband. This was in 2002, eight years after the first family violence law was implemented. The state's inaction in the face of Luz's experiences of domestic violence proved to be life-threatening. At that time, she was not enough of a citizen to be heard or to have her case dealt with in a timely manner.

"I don't believe in this democracy. No, absolutely not," she told me.

Luz was disillusioned by the state's lack of response to her cries for help when she feared for her life, but also more widely by the state's foundations in the neoliberal economic model. The powerful wanted to display an image of Chile to the world as an example of the successes of the neoliberal model, she told me. Meanwhile, in the schools, "the libraries [are] closed. The computers do not have the adequate programs. . . . It is only an image. I feel that it is an image." Luz criticized the institutionalization of art, culture, and social movements during democracy. This came out clearly in her critique of SERNAM in 2003:

> SERNAM in my opinion is another element that the government constructed in order to seem like a modern government, a modern state, the same ones who approve conventions and don't even read them, human rights conventions. . . . The same women who work in SERNAM were women who fought a lot. . . . They know what women need. They know. . . . But they sold themselves to the model [i.e., neoliberal model]. They feel like [that way] they can do something. . . . Because they don't have resources. . . . Have you heard of SERNAM having a seminar about abortion? . . . No, no they have never done that, or about divorce. But they talk about violence. They make a poster about a woman with a black eye, and everything is on the surface. It is so as not to break the equilibrium. People really fear breaking the equilibrium, as if this democracy is so fragile that it could fall apart.

In August 2003, barely a year after her husband's attempt to murder her, Luz elaborated on her critique of the postdictatorship government as we rode on a bus filled with grassroots women's groups across town toward Parque por la Paz Villa Grimaldi, which is a memorial to those the state tortured and killed there during the dictatorship. The women's groups had organized a trip there in honor of the thirtieth anniversary of the coup of September 11, 1973. Luz told me as we bumped along that she was disillusioned with the myriad television shows commemorating the thirtieth anniversary of the coup, including the countless popular television documentaries of the events surrounding the bombing of La Moneda, the presidential palace. Newsstands displayed front pages and special issues of *La Nación*, *El Mercurio*, *The Clinic*, and other widely read newspapers, dedicated to commemorating the coup, mostly focused on mourning and recuperating the memory of those who were its victims and heroes, especially President Salvador Allende, who died during the coup. Luz was critical of the popular and superficial treatment the coup received in the media. She preferred

real action, deep commemoration, and social change to constant media representations and appropriations of the events, which had lasting
impacts on individuals, families, and society.

Our two guides to Villa Grimaldi that chilly August afternoon in
2003 had survived the state's torture at the site, and they took grassroots
women's groups and me on a moving walk through the memorial. The
woman who guided us told us about the gendered dimensions of captivity. Women were raped, their feminine gender roles used against
them. Sometimes, she said, their children were brought in and made
to watch while their mothers were raped and tortured. Our other guide
told us about the everyday "torture" of constantly being blindfolded.
He explained that when the International Red Cross toured the site
to investigate suspicions of torture, the prisoners were forced to hide
in an empty pool, covered by a tarp, so that the Red Cross could not
confirm these allegations. We walked through "the Tower," where they
took prisoners condemned to death. Four or five prisoners were held
there in a small cupboard-like space, knowing that most of them would
not come out alive.

At the end of the tour, we all gathered in a beautifully decorated
plaza, which had been used by agents of the dictatorial state decades
earlier, as a disciplinary space where they ran over people's limbs with
vehicles, mangling and destroying their hands, feet, legs, and arms
while other prisoners watched. On that afternoon in late winter 2003
Luz and I, along with the other women of the women's grassroots collective, held hands and some of the women spoke. Someone brought
red carnations so that we could each choose sites to place them, in me-
moriam and in solidarity. A dedicated grassroots women's rights activist and former *orientadora* at Safe Space lamented to me that the act
in which we were engaged that day was all too rare. Chileans make
long pilgrimages to all kinds of religious sites, she pointed out, but not
to memorials of the dictatorship's terror. Once again, I noted, women
were linking their own rights as women with the struggle for rights during and following the dictatorial regime.

By the time I met with Luz in 2009, she was politically aware in
another way, now that she was working directly with poor women on

Figure 4. Posters such as these, glued to a building wall in Santiago around
the thirtieth anniversary of the coup, dotted the city. The man in the photos is
Salvador Allende. The posters say: "30 years after the coup, we demand truth
and justice." The crowd in the picture holds a banner demanding: "No to
Impunity." They are holding up pictures of those disappeared and tortured by the
dictatorship. The poster underneath advertises a march on September 11 at La
Moneda, the presidential palace demolished during the coup. (Photograph by the
author, 2009)

gender-related issues in her position within the national government.
She complained:

> The offices don't have adequate funding. They don't train the officials
> adequately. We are critical . . . and what happens is that . . . where the
> opposition is in charge [i.e., where the mayor is part of the opposing
> political party, Alianza por Chile], they don't let you in. So you can't
> work in that borough. The boroughs where we can work are [led by]
> Concertación governments.

The local governments "are the owners of the place," she said. For
Luz, the devolution of power to municipal governments, enacted by
Pinochet, has provided a way to "maintain control over the population.

It is a form of control and manipulation, because health and educational services are there . . . the funds for the social organizations. The projects for the social organizations [nongovernmental organizations] go through the municipality. . . . In this way, we need a revolution." Luz felt that citizens participate only in activities that are allowed by the authorities. "Because it's all regulated in this country, everything," she said.

She elaborated on this thought, which resonates with Josefina's complaint that "the joy never came": "Sure, the organizations and groups, the path is participation, but it's a closed path. . . . Pinochet did this, but the Concertación reaffirmed it. . . . [T]he Concertación comes and reinforces the mechanisms and uses them to maintain themselves, nothing else." Although participation in government was encouraged, the government severely limited the forms of that participation, according to Luz. In Luz's narrated conception of herself, she works against not only constraining gender roles, but also class inequality, because she sees gender and class subordination as intersecting aspects of her subjectivity.[3]

Mullings (2006) has emphasized that race, class, and gender are not preexisting identities; racism, sexism, and classism are active, interactional processes that shape women's lives and their health. Luz's experiences of the intersections of gender and class, and her resistance to hegemonic, dominant models of how she should be as a woman from a poor background, come through strongly in her narrative. Her roots in the lower-middle class constitute one of the most important sources of her strength. She described herself as having been "a poor woman who was raised in a *población*." She was very aware of her class status. She told me, "My children were also raised in the same poverty. Now my children are professionals. I am super proud of that. . . . Together we broke out. We made a break with that history of more poverty, more pain, and we were able to transform that into something different."

Luz's three children were able to study in the university because they won scholarships and took out loans, without which they would not have been able to attend, Luz explained, because, "We didn't have *plata* [money]. We were so poor." Here, Luz pointedly claimed her class position as a poor woman, but she quickly made sure to tell me that her motivation for her children to obtain university educations was not related to a quest for upward class mobility:

> No, it's not for that. It's for harmony. . . . A position in life, with a goal. In the search to do something that is really important, not to allow oneself to get swept away, with the idea that nothing is possible, [that] "I have to be a manual laborer, earn a miserable wage." It's different.

She said, "Imagine, [my son], all of the children that he played with . . . they are delinquents [now that they are adults]. They take drugs. Some are drivers. . . . One has a truck, another a taxi. That's how it is." Luz derives a lot of her strength from the professional successes of her children. In spite of the abuse and in spite of her history of poverty, her children have a different life, and this made her very proud.

Sanación through Transformative Ties

> Research on gender and violence is not only about
> how worlds are unmade by violence but also how
> they are remade. —Veena Das (2008:293)

While listening to the twists and turns Luz's life had taken and how she now narrated them, I was attentive to the relationship between how she framed her experiences in her 2009 narrative and how she framed them in 2003. Listening to her in 2009 I was struck by her resilience and how her resilience was a powerful form of agency. She then framed her life history in terms of *sanación* [healing], which seems to signify for her resilience, recuperation, strength, and recovery. "I always had it, you know? I always had that strength. I always had it," she said to me.

Rather than the term "aftermath," commonly used for victims of extreme events, Gomez-Barris (2009), in her analysis of the effects of Chilean political violence on the lives and memories of Chileans, proposes the term "afterlife" as a better way to understand those effects. Although she applies afterlife to the effects of political violence, this term also aptly applies to the effects of intimate partner violence. Gomez-

Barris proposes that "the *afterlife* of political violence [consists of] the continuing and persistent symbolic and material effects of the original event of violence on people's daily lives, their social and psychic identities, and their ongoing wrestling with the past in the present" (6).

Luz took me through some of the processes of her remembering in her afterlife. This act of rendering her life story to me constituted a form of agency and allowed her to critique and remake her embodiment of the symbolic violence of gender inequality (Bourdieu 2001, 1990; see also Reed-Danahay 2005). Luz explained that she felt she had to engage in an excavation of herself to find the roots of the violence and how it had lodged inside herself, as poisonous knowledge, in order to modify those roots to fit with her newfound nonviolent self. Her self-analysis and reworking were deeply intersubjective and embedded within the varying contexts in which she operated. By 2009, Luz framed her acts of remembering and excavating the violence of the past and present in terms of gender socialization, expectations, performances, and inequalities as crucial to her self-defined project of *sanación*.

Sanación, Luz explained, was characterized by her engagement in activities that contribute to her reclaiming of herself and remaking meaning in her life. Luz explained to me that "*para sanarte* [to heal oneself], there has to be something to repair." Her project, as she described it, constitutes a form of agency and an attempt to redefine "gender," to remake gendered expectations and the violence of gendered expectations based in inequality. As she looked back over her life, she perceived that the various forms of gendered violence she experienced throughout her lifetime "poisoned" (Das 2008) her own way of thinking and infected her interactions with other people. She told me:

> I even lowered my tone of voice because I felt it was violent. I changed
> my way of thinking. . . . Because I also felt responsible for this level of
> violence, also my conduct with my children, with my family, because
> I was very disruptive. I always went for the confrontation. I changed
> all of that. But I think that is also part of the *sanación*, realizing for
> oneself, becoming conscious of the reality that everything is violence.

Everything is aggressive, violent . . . a way of relating to others. . . .
[One has] to be very attentive to perceiving violence in all of its forms.

Gendered expectations are socially produced, reproduced, and critiqued in Luz's interactions with family members, friends, and medical
and judicial authorities. Recoveries—the forms they take, how they are
defined by those who suffer, and what they mean—are intersubjective.
For Luz, this intersubjectivity is both local and global. I use the term
"recovery" here carefully, to mean the processes in which people engage to transform some form or forms of damage they have suffered.
Such transformations are processes, and the efforts to reconstitute
meaning in the face of life-changing events are ongoing (Becker 1997;
Luborsky 1994). For Luz, the transformation of gender roles is central
to her sense of recovering herself, of moving beyond the acceptable
gender role position as a "victim" of domestic violence.

Sanación and Transforming Gender

In contrast to the ways in which her family, health care providers, and
judicial systems upheld dominant gender role expectations based on
women's inequality, Luz's interactions with the globally connected domestic violence organization Safe Space, which emphasized women's
rights, along with her participation in other such organizations and in a
global movement of women's spirituality circles, allowed her to engage
in processes of *sanación*, as she called it in 2009. I refer to the relationships Luz has formed over the years through these groups as *transformative ties*.[4]

Luz first began to identify the role of gender inequality in her experiences of violence through her participation at Safe Space, which began in 2000. For her this was a turning point. A friend from a women's
organization to which Luz belonged made an appointment for her at
Safe Space. At first, Luz did not want to go because of the negative experiences she had had with therapeutic professionals in the past, but
she felt obliged because of her friend's effort.

Luz told me in 2003 that at Safe Space she began to learn language that allowed her to name the various forms of violence she suffered and to understand the violence in broader terms. She attended group therapy sessions where she formed transformative ties that allowed her to see beyond gender role expectations based in women's inequality:

> I felt terribly bad, to hear the other women in the group talking and to hear the same atrocities that were happening to me and the same discomforts. But . . . I felt different. I always had a sensation that I was different. Because they cried and fussed, and I said, "I don't have any reason to cry. I don't have any reason to feel pain. . . . It was the life I chose." Do you understand? I was very firm in that. I chose this, . . . and they cried, and they told me, "Hey, but it can't be . . . that you, how you are!" It was a questioning among us because I questioned them, and they questioned me, and things started to emerge. I started to talk about things, the fights, the problems [*dramas*] that I had.

The effects of these intersubjective engagements with other women who had suffered domestic violence and professionals attuned to the problem at Safe Space were very different from those she had experienced in her prior help-seeking in medical settings years before. Luz described some of the positive outcomes of those therapeutic sessions, based in an ideology of women's equality and citizenship rights:

> It was very important because I was able to realize that it wasn't necessary that I have such a bad time. . . . I started to realize all of those things, that moreover . . . because of my condition [i.e., her homosexuality], I suffered those things and arrived at the conclusion that it was a self-punishment or a form of . . . sacrificing myself . . . for what I felt or how I was. I sacrificed myself by dealing with my husband because he maintained my status as a woman with children, a husband, with a house. . . . For me this started to become clear. I started to realize. I did everything as a process, although the therapy was for violence, I started to do personal work there, to understand, and it was accompanied by this women's citizenship workshop. It was . . . everything together.

Luz told me when we talked in 2003 that she still kept in touch with four other women from the group therapy who provided support for one another. Because of the activities in which she engaged through Safe Space, Luz explained, "I started to think that I . . . had the right to do with my life [what I wanted] . . . to change my life, to do other things," and she decided to make radical changes in her life. She stopped taking her pills, started going out for fun and to seminars, and began taking better care of herself. She was also elected director of the Women's Place.

In 2009, many years after our original conversations, which took place in 2003, Luz's transformational work, her *sanación*, continued and now entailed conversing with a close-knit group of friends about her suffering and healing. Luz's group, a friendship circle of women, constitutes what she describes as her form of spirituality and was inspired by the work of US psychiatrist Jean Bolen in her book *The Millionth Circle: How to Change Ourselves and the World; The Essential Guide to Women's Circles* (1999). Bolen is a renowned psychiatrist who has worked at the University of California–San Francisco and has been recognized as a distinguished scholar by the American Psychiatric Association. She is an advocate for a United Nations Fifth World Conference on Women because she believes that women, working from the grassroots, hold the keys to saving humankind from the various forms of violence that human beings have waged on the earth and each other.

Luz gave me a printed copy of the book, which had been translated into Spanish by a Venezuelan woman and disseminated through the Internet, another way in which globalization is inseparable from Luz's experiences of *sanación*.

"With these women friends I have, when we get together, we take care of one another [*contenernos*], and things can be said," she told me.

Luz's circle of women serves—as Safe Space groups did in the past—simultaneously as a kind of kinship of affliction and a kinship of affinity. It replaces for Luz her ruptured bonds with her family of origin and her friends, who did not support her in her quest to find a way to live her life beyond constraining gender roles, marriage, motherhood, and heterosexuality.

The Millionth Circle[5]

Western civilization is the story of patriarchy,
a dominator, hierarchical history of power and intellect
that together have brought us to new heights of technology,
and to the possibility of destroying our planet.
Our rain forests are being slashed and burned.
Our air, land and water polluted.
Nuclear waste, ground poisoning chemicals,
hydrocarbons and toxic aerosols
poison our Mother Earth
ourselves, and all creatures great and small.
Toxicity and indifference
damage chromosomes, make holes in the ozone
result in air so thick many gasp and cough
as they breathe.
Profit and power as the ruling principles,
lead to this
and to wars.
Are creating a wasteland.
A peaceful revolution is going on,
a women's spirituality revolution, hidden in plain sight.
Through circles of women, healing women,
Might the culture come around?
(Bolen 1999:81–82)

Luz explained to me that this form of spirituality is a way to claim power for herself and for women more generally. In claiming a new identity for herself, outside of her roles as a mother and wife subservient to others' needs, Luz felt that she had risked her life and her social networks. She was able to do so because she engaged with new networks of women, such as those at Safe Space and other women's organizations. These groups linked her to global women's rights issues and social activism of various kinds. She connects her *sanación* to local organizations, both formal and informal, and to global frameworks originating elsewhere and disseminated through the tools of globalization.

Against Victimhood

A fundamental aspect of Luz's *sanación*, growing out of these local and global transformative ties, is her identification of the victim role as the fundamental gendered role against which she constructs her identity. Although she has suffered, she is not a victim; this is fundamental to her self-concept. She explained why her life project of claiming an identity beyond gender constraints has been so important for her: "In this country it is very strong the model of the Virgin, the Virgin Mary. . . . It's very strong. It's very idealized. The Catholic Church has taken charge of installing in us the image of purity, of victimization, of suffering, of abnegation."

Luz believed that Chilean women have this role of suffering and self-sacrifice so deeply integrated into their sense of themselves that they respond to the suffering of domestic violence by saying, "That's life," and then continuing on. This normalized condition of victimhood is core to many women's internalized gender roles based on their own subordination. Luz explained:

The society makes you a victim. And moreover, the women who work on domestic violence, they make victims. . . . That gets closer to the model of what they expect of you. It's internalized in women. . . . The same women who are working on these problems, I am sure that they have gone through a process of development. They understand things [but] when you start to look into it, they are [also] victims themselves. They are victims. . . . They are victims of the organization because they "have to do everything." They are so self-sacrificing. Last night they were "working until midnight." It's like part of being a woman in Chile, the condition of being a "victim." Probably others think they are doing you a favor [by saying to a woman who has been abused], "Poor thing, what happened to her."

The very basis of living as a woman is suffering so that others may have a better life. The basis of a woman's personhood, then, is her denial of herself. Ironically, in order to be a social being and to avoid the threat of social abandonment (Biehl 2005), women must in a sense deny themselves—deny their self-development. This is a kind of death of the self, as it encourages women to negate themselves, to deny their full personhood in order to legitimately claim social personhood. For Luz, the victim role is a gendered and debilitated role, marked by a lack of power, against which she constructs her identity.

In many interviews and conversations during my research, women described the victim role as a fundamental aspect of gendered identity for women. Marisol had to embody the role in order to obtain her rights from the judicial system (see Chapters 3 and 4). The idea that women actually enjoy suffering is prevalent, as shown in a newsmagazine article about "masochistic depression" (Egert 2002). I posit that the "victim role" is a nonthreatening, submissive, and socially acceptable way for women to express the dissatisfaction and suffering produced by inequalities because it is consonant with common ideas about women's acceptable roles and does not therefore substantively call into question the status quo of gender inequality.[6] Indeed, professionals working in the field of domestic violence have suggested that the state's responses to domestic violence, including the recently instituted safe houses (*casas de acogida*), reinforce the existing patriarchal order, which works against women's escape from domestic violence and their self-definition of and engagement in recovery processes (SERNAM et al. 2007).

Luz continued in this regard:

I think we women maintain this pattern in this country, saying "that's life." Chilean women are such fighters, so persistent [*empeñosas*], so hard-working [*esforzadas*]. We're good. Some time before this episode [attempted murder], I was realizing who I really was, because to be able to make that leap I had to say, "No. That's it. I can't do it anymore." *It was like thinking that I wasn't so good.* Like saying, "No, I can't keep worrying about my family. He has to take charge of his life. My children are older. Let the world take care of itself. I want to get my life in order." . . . Many people told me, "You went too far [*te pasaste*]. No woman would have done that. You broke the mold. You put yourself first and went to the other extreme." Very troublesome and very threatening for other women.

Because Luz had gone "too far," many women blamed her for her husband's act of extreme violence against her in 2002. She explained, "It was like a justification. [They would say,] 'You know, nobody would have been able to handle what you wanted to do [which was to leave him]. It was obvious that he had to react like that.'"

> Women who are feminists told me . . ."Go back to the house. Calm down." . . . It's deeply rooted. In all contexts. For women who have studied it, it's outside of them. Not inside. . . . In the organizations where I participated, it [i.e., her wanting to leave him] was too much for them.
>
> The woman is like the pillar of the family. I am telling you, it tires you. The family tires you, keeping everyone afloat. And you change. You are not recognizable anymore. Because you changed your way of thinking, of seeing. And that is very complicated. And then, when this thing happened [the shooting] I start to examine everything for violence. Everything is violent. . . .
>
> The woman has to keep herself in a situation or a way of acting so that the violence doesn't explode, which is worse. Because of that it depends on the woman. If you don't complain, if you're not demanding, if you don't make demands, there's no violence and everything stays the same. But if you make demands, if you complain, if you say, "No, that's it," and everything, the psychologists, everyone says that is the most dangerous moment for violence. The biggest risk one runs is when you say, "No. That's it. Stop it."

Although the changes Luz wished to see have been slow in coming, she cultivated various forums where she can speak about and work toward enacting the changes that she wants to see and experience. In effect, she had risked her life to bring about these changes for herself. Her life depended on it. Her sense of herself depended on it. Prior to making those changes, she felt she "wasn't living." What is life if you feel like you are not living? Is it still life?

Luz reclaimed a subjectivity outside of the victim role. She emphasized this to me as she constructed her narrative and sense of herself.

> I try not to look at it from the role of the victim . . . or of a poor woman. . . . I don't accept that. . . . Imagine if you told someone, "I interviewed a woman who survived, lived twenty-four years with a man, and in the end what happened, poor woman." But no, it was one fact of my life. It's like I have isolated it and left it behind. Of course it marked my life. It has done a lot of harm. A lot of things happened that shouldn't have. But, *basically I have recovered who I am.*

Here, Luz refuses the gendered victim role in favor of constructing her identity, her self, and her life around the idea of being a strong woman, a woman who was able to get out of a violent relationship and who is doing well on her own.

The process of telling her story has been for Luz a part of her process of self-realization and transformation. Indeed, Lamb (2001:28) notes that "the telling of stories is one of the practices by which people reflect, exercise agency, contest interpretations of things, make meanings, feel sorrow and hope, and live their lives" (cited in Brettell 2003:24; see also Maynes et al. 2008).

Conclusion: Resilience as Agency

Luz conceptualized her healing activities in concert with other women engaged in the same work of remaking meaning for themselves and society, both locally and globally. From her perspective, these spheres are bound together. Through these efforts, Luz created new meaning and recreated gendered roles and expectations for herself. In a way, it seems that Luz wishes to live beyond gender, that is, to inhabit a subjectivity that is not encased and determined by gendered expectations, but is structured by forms of self-development that are unhinged from such expectations and are therefore in process and up for interpretation.

In Luz's processes of *sanación*, she engaged in identifying what has been seen as normal and everyday life for women but is actually abuse. As Das (2008:283) has pointed out, "Violence, far from being an interruption in the ordinary, is folded into the ordinary." Luz excavates the ordinary by bringing the abuses out of invisibility, bringing them to language, and naming them as part of her experience of violence. She practices a form of agency in her critical reflections on and excavations of "the ordinary." In that process, she names and thereby reworks the symbolic violence of gender inequality that underlies much of social, political, and economic life (Scheper-Hughes and Bourgois 2004). Marisol, too, has consistently reminded me that for her it is necessary to do the work of making domestic violence visible, of naming it, in order to reorder individual and social lives.

Luz's generation of new affective ties with other women—women in the various groups to which she belongs, and now especially in her women's spirituality circle—allowed her to transform herself. In this way, Luz engaged in what Das has described as the swallowing of "poisonous knowledge." Das (2008:294) "considers the manner in which women engage in repair of relationships through the ordinary, everyday acts of caring [and] thinks of healing through the metaphor of women digesting 'poisonous' knowledge so that they learn to reinhabit the world by dwelling again within internal landscapes devastated by violence." As Das has suggested, Luz has figured out a way, through her transformative ties, to "reinhabit the world" in a new way. As part of Luz's reworking of poisonous knowledge, she works toward social change so that her society, both local and global, might one day resemble more of herself, and therefore enable her to reinhabit the world— both local and global—more fully on her own terms.

Sanación, as Luz calls her form of recovery, occurs outside the gaze of the state (see Das and Poole 2004). Although women need different tools to engage in their own processes of recovery from domestic violence, this fact has remained largely illegible to the state. Luz's recovery and experiences can be conceptualized as emerging from the tension between agency and structure, wherein she has been able to create new possibilities for a regendered or even a nongendered sense of herself. Luz creates changes within herself and within the world so that her recovered sense of self, of subjectivity, will have a home in the world. This notion of healing through changing the world runs counter to the neoliberal move toward psychotherapy as a form of self-governance (Merry 2006). It is a form of remaking and reordering— growing out of the poisonous soil of intimate violence. Luz's journey is shaped in part by her agentive acts, geared toward propelling herself into the future to create a meaningful, fulfilled life, not by forgetting but by reshaping the meaning of the violence and engaging in transformative acts with other women.

Luz's *sanación* is a way for her to claim what is hers—her body and herself—the most fundamental sites of gendered domination by the state and by abusive men in intimate relationships. Her life project of *sanación* is about transforming herself and thereby transforming social orders, and doing so in a way that is creative of new orders, not merely in opposition to historically entrenched social hierarchies.[7] Through *sanación* Luz's suffering is made meaningful. It is transmuted into something else. Even still, in a way the marks of violence are indelible, and the poisonous knowledge violence produced for her, while it can be transformed, still moves her subjective experience.

CHAPTER 6

Contingencies of Care

There is always the goal of continuing to
construct democracy in the country and
the home. —SERNAM official, 2009

Late one night in 2007, in the middle of a major multilane traffic artery
in Santiago, a man brutally beat a woman unconscious, leaving her
there. A bystander used his cell-phone camera to record the horrific
scene, and *Terra*, a Chilean Internet-based news site, later reported on
it. In the video we see the woman lying helplessly in the middle of
the road, unconscious, with cars whizzing past, coming close to running her over, as two police officers watch, their hands stuffed into
their pockets. Another officer arrives and also just observes the scene.
The state, embodied in these three officers, utterly and blatantly failed
to act, even as the abuse unfolded before its agents' eyes. Eventually
the woman regained consciousness, and the violence continued. The
Terra reporter narrated:

> The woman again gets to her feet. The aggressor grabs her by the arm
> and makes her cross the street and hits her repeatedly again, this time
> against a wall of the police station. . . . Only 30 meters from the station
> the woman receives the final blow. At this point, she is not moving, is
> apparently unconscious, and her aggressor leaves the scene quickly.
> Finally, this abused woman goes away with an unknown person.
> There is no record of an ambulance in the area, or of a woman in any
> hospital that morning for such injuries.

A man had blatantly beaten a woman with whom he apparently had
some sort of intimate relationship, given their initial embrace. He had
beaten her repeatedly in front of three police officers who colluded

with the abuse by failing to intervene. In effect, they granted the aggressor impunity as they willingly averted their gaze to the violence being done.

After *Terra* made these events public the Chilean state finally reacted and expelled the policemen who had willingly failed to act while witnessing a woman being beaten. In the end, the state upheld its promises of gender equity and intervention on behalf of women who suffer gender-based violence. But the incident had happened. It could not be erased.

We are left to wonder: Where did this woman go after she was so viciously wounded? How was she affected by the cruel public beatings and the indifference of the authorities when she was living by a thread? This incident represents the precariousness of the state's care for women who suffer gender-based violence. Here, care was contingent on the actions of the police as officials of the state charged with enacting its laws. No care was provided here, except, perhaps, by the innocent bystander who recorded the events on her or his camera phone and then sent it to *Terra*, who then in turn used its Internet platform to circulate the images within and beyond Chile.

The inaction of the police in this instance represents a blatant and violent lack of care on the part of the state, a lack of care that produced harm. Many other forms of care for women who suffer gender-based violence are also contingent and cause further suffering. This chapter examines various ways in which Family Care, Safe Space, and SERNAM's forms of care, while at times healing, have also been contingent in ways that can cause harm (see also Ticktin 2011).

Contingent Care

Marisol's, Josefina's, and Luz's processes of recovery, like their life situations, have been very different from one another. The kinds of care they have accessed are diverse, and their emotional and material situations and needs have mirrored this diversity. They often expressed frustration at the lack of care they received. They sought care related to their mental and physical health, yet the forms of care doled out by government officials, including police, lawyers, and social workers, often failed to meet their real needs. Often, their interactions with such state officials left them dissatisfied and feeling more vulnerable, a paradoxical by-product of the process of legislating and bureaucratizing care for women who suffer intimate partner violence. In the process of boiling down and "packaging" suffering to make it legible to institutions of care, an ethic of care sometimes is lost or misplaced, whether intentionally or not.

We have already seen, in Marisol's narrative, how care is contingent on the performance of the "good victim" role. The "care" she received in the judicial system was predicated on her ability and willingness to perform her role as a "victim" time and again to prove in the eyes of the state that she merited its interventions. This is not therefore "fake" care, nor a complete lack of care. Instead, it is a form of contingent care that is built on the neoliberal ethic of self-responsibility and self-efficacy rather than on an ethic of care. It is a legislated, bureaucratized form of care within the neoliberal economic state. We have also seen in the narratives of Marisol, Josefina, and Luz how care is contingent on a person's ability and willingness to seek out help repeatedly. Much as Biehl (2007) shows in the case of poor AIDS sufferers in Brazil, care depends on a person's ability and willingness to "activate" the state. Especially for women who are traumatized and stigmatized by intimate partner violence, the possibilities to activate the state in order to gain its forms of care are at times out of reach, as some women feel entitled while others do not. A sense of rights and the entitlement to claim them is thus a prerequisite to accessing the state's forms of care.

Safe Space, Family Care, and SERNAM all have provided precarious and constantly shifting forms of care that have been contingent to a large degree on political will and the dedication of economic resources at local, regional, and national levels. Uncertainty about resources and political battles over the contours of available care suck resources and energy from the very agencies and professionals who provide care. At times, even the survival of institutions dedicated to domestic violence work is at stake, shaping their agendas in ways that distort and divert attention and resources from the women who seek their care. During my ethnographic research there, I observed how Safe Space and Family Care dealt with these contingencies in different ways.

"Women Have the Right to Quality Care!"
Safe Space and Political-Economic Contingencies of Care

> I am more and more convinced that the most political act you can perform is to take your body to the street.
> —Ema, August 2011, following a student movement protest where we were sprayed with CS tear gas, after which we participated in a *cacerolazo*[1]

The Public Hearing

A din of voices filled the municipality's multipurpose room on a warm spring night in 2003 for a public hearing, a mechanism instituted during the official transition to democracy to increase citizen participation in municipality governance. Various women's groups, including Safe Space, had demanded the public hearing to protest the municipality's slashing of funding for nongovernmental agencies that had provided care for women who had suffered domestic violence. The packed space and energy of the crowd at the public hearing made it hot and humid with perspiration. Several groups dotted the walls at the public hearing with handmade posters highlighting some of their demands for the mayor and city council.[2] At intervals, waves of chanting welled up from the crowd. "Consciousness, memory, women!" they shouted in unison. "Let's go! Let's go, women! This evening they have to listen to us!" "Mayor, we have stopped believing your thousands of promises!" I knew that many women involved in the protest that night came to adulthood in the 1980s, protesting the dictatorial regime and advocating for women's rights. They were well practiced in the art of political protest.

In this uncomfortable but electrified government building, women once again forced the gendered, private suffering of intimate relation-

Figure 5. This poster called for "Security in the Home." By invoking the political claims to women's equality made by the women's rights movement during the transition to democracy under their slogan "Democracy in the Country and in the Home," this poster seemed to critique the elision of domestic violence in the relatively new discourse of "citizen safety." (Photograph by the author, 2003)

ships into the arena of the state. They spoke publicly of pain. They spoke publicly against pain. Speaking of pain is a highly political act, and at that point they had more than a decade of work on the now-public issue of domestic violence to draw from in their expressions of pain; they spoke publicly about pain's complicated social etiologies and demanded palliatives for the pain.

Lila was the first woman who had endured domestic violence to address the crowd. I knew part of Lila's story already, since we had met twice at Safe Space for her to share her life history narrative with me. In her late twenties, she was the youngest woman I interviewed.

"I'm a little nervous," Lila started out timidly. Indeed, she was quite notably nervous as she stood at the dais in front of the crowd and next to the mayor and city council. "I have never been in front of so many people," she told us.

"I am twenty-eight years old. . . . I am going to give my testimony: 'What Safe Space did for me,'" she told the crowd.

Then, Lila began to cry.

"Go ahead, woman!" (*Arriba mujer!*), yelled the audience, clapping in encouragement.

"When Safe Space had the support of the mayor," Lila continued, quite painfully, her emotions raw and exposed, "Safe Space gave me the strength to move forward, with two daughters." Through her tears she insisted on continuing her testimony:

> I suffered a lot of psychological abuse, physical abuse, but thanks to the people at Safe Space, I moved forward. Now I can say with pride that although some marks have remained—still when I remember, my soul hurts—I can say that I am a happy woman. And you know why? Because that which women sometimes lose came back to me, the pride of being a mother. I felt that I was a woman who was worthless. . . . I felt that I wasn't good for anything. And Safe Space, through their psychologist, gave me strength to feel proud of being a mother and raising two daughters as I am doing now. I feel proud of all the people who work at Safe Space because they continue helping me. They don't have many resources but when I tell them about a problem, unconditionally and from their own pockets, they have given support for my daughters and my home. Thanks to them and the lawyer at Safe Space, I won the trial for family violence. I had been abused, beaten and a lot of other things, humiliated, and thanks to them I have gotten a lot of things, the strength to go on and have relationships with people . . . to realize that I too, [have value as a] mother, as a person, as a woman. And I ask, Mr. Mayor, if you really have a heart . . . that you authorize for Safe Space, what Safe Space really needs, for all of the women who are here now.

After Lila spoke, other women took turns giving their testimonies about the importance of the municipality's support of women's agencies that had provided care in the past but could no longer do so after the municipality cut their funding.

Marisol—who had invited me to the public hearing—Luz, and Ema were all part of the large, boisterous crowd of mostly women that night, as were other women who had worked or received care at Safe Space. The municipal government had redirected its funds away from Safe Space and other such agencies to the new municipality-run Family Treatment Center, which was focused on an ideology of "the family" as a heterosexual, nuclear unit with mother as caretaker of the family and the family's image, not a family based on gender equality. Marisol eventually sought help at the Family Treatment Center because in 2006, when Gerardo reappeared in Chile, Safe Space no longer offered care (see Chapter 3). Ema explained to me that without supplemental funding from the municipality, Safe Space simply was not able to provide direct care for women.

Here, through the mechanism of the public hearing, Safe Space was able to publically protest the loss of their direct care program, which had been based (even though not explicitly) in feminist ethics of care. In this space, creativity emerged as both a form of agency and political power, showing some of "the possibilities and the limits of the creativity of everyday life" (Das 2001:27). It was an instance of collective creativity or, more specifically, *collective, gendered creativity* (see also Ahearn 2001). Forms of gendered collective agency, asserted through political mobilization, emerged before the eyes of the municipality's leaders, forcing into visibility a different model of intervention in domestic violence, even if only for a brief moment (see Stark 2007:195) and without tangible effect. Safe Space's model of intervention in gender-based violence encompassed a new vision of state and society. In this new vision citizens' voices are heard and considered and gender equity is central. Fundamental structures of inequality embedded in state and society, and forms of structural violence that intersect with domestic violence are addressed. The solutions to the problem of gender-based violence, as well its etiologies, are seen as social.

In spite of this assertion of a collective, gendered agency that Safe Space and others exerted during the public hearing, the municipality did not budge. The mayor stormed out about thirty minutes into the hearing, angry with the unruly audience who would not succumb to his authority, which they were calling into question. When he left, taking the microphones with him, the hearing fell apart.

My entanglements in events surrounding the public hearing that night reflected my situation as an ethnographer involved in "deep play" (Geertz 1973). That night, I became an insider in a way that allowed me to see more of the political-economic contexts in which Safe Space and other women's rights organizations operated and the stakes that were involved. After the mayor's departure there was commotion around the auditorium door as many people left. Marisol encouraged me to go outside to take pictures of what was happening there, indicating it could be of interest. There, I encountered a few women harassing the women's rights protestors, and I decided that since it was a public event, I would take a picture of them as well, as I had been doing in plain sight all night inside the auditorium. One of the women who was harassing the women's rights protestors saw me take a picture that included her, warned me fiercely not to do so, and then lunged at me, tugging at the camera that was around my neck. Two police officers looked on, quite unsurprised and unconcerned about her physical attack on me. They did nothing. As a crowd gathered around us, I was afraid of being hurt, so I took the camera strap from my neck and stopped fighting the woman for it. She took the camera, which soon ended up in the police van that was outside the auditorium. Eventually, Marisol, Luz, and some of the other women I knew through Safe Space came to support me as I was escorted upstairs to a city council room where a city council member tried to dissuade me from pressing charges, which I insisted upon doing anyway.

At about that same time, the mayor was appearing on a television talk show to enjoy *pisco sours* (an alcoholic beverage made with *pisco*, a grape-based brandy, and lemon juice) and an *asado* (barbecue), while discussing current events in a light-hearted manner. Showing his disdain for the women's rights organizations and the mechanism of the public hearing that he had left only an hour prior, the mayor classified the event as a "catfight" between "his women," the women who supported him, and "the local representative's women," who "belonged to" the popular congressional representative who consistently supported women's rights in his district. The mayor later publicly asserted that I had been the "gringa" who had started all of the problems, leading to the attack on me. Colleagues later assured me that I was merely asserting my rights to take photographs at a public event. The mayor consistently defended his treatment of the women's rights organizations, including Safe Space, saying that he worked "tirelessly" to defend women in his municipality because women are the fundamental pillars of the Chilean family and nation. He was, then, defending the historically entrenched gender ideologies that enforce women's subordination in family and society—precisely the ones that Safe Space and other women's rights organizations protested at the public hearing.

When the case about the attack on me at the public hearing went to court, Marisol met me there, as did Luz, as a witness on my behalf. After hearing both sides, the judge informed me (here I paraphrase): "You have to understand that there was a military regime here for many years, and we are very sensitive about people coming in from outside and taking pictures," emphasizing my position as an outsider who could never really understand the local context. "It is only natural that when people get angry, they resort to violence," he calmly explained to me.

Once the witnesses had spoken and we had minimally responded, the judge encouraged us to come to an agreement, a reconciliation, which I was eager to do. The woman who had attacked me, who appeared to be without many resources, asked me for an apology for having taken pictures of her. I conceded to her request because, although legally I was within my rights, I was sorry that she had been offended and angered by my pictures (in fact, I had destroyed the negatives while at the police station the night of the public hearing, as a good faith measure). I was especially sorry once I realized that it was likely she had been paid by the mayor's supporters to disrupt the event on his behalf, thus indicating her class-based subordination. In return, I asked for her apology for having attacked me, which she refused to give, so I decided not to terminate the case there and instead requested the next step, which was for the judge to decide the outcome. I was to receive notification of his decision within three months, but it never arrived.

In light of the municipality's cuts to Safe Space's funding for direct care, cuts that remained in place after the public hearing, Safe Space shifted toward research, and care for women who suffered domestic violence was centralized in the bureaucracies of the municipality, most notably in the new Family Treatment Center. Soon after, Safe Space relocated to another municipality, where it pursued its work with funding primarily from other countries and international agencies. By 2009 Safe Space was once again offering services to women who suffered domestic violence, though a few days after I arrived, they suffered another huge blow, an unforeseen contingency. Thugs had broken into their offices, leaving the heavy wooden front door axed apart, digital databases destroyed, computer cords cut, and windows smashed. Ema explained that it was likely the drug-dealing husband of one of their clients who was responsible. Here was another form of contingency that required Safe Space's programs and efforts to shift.

"The Good Treatment Campaign": Family Care's Political-Economic Contingencies

By 2001 Family Care's program for women who suffered domestic violence was also in danger of being closed down by a newly elected mayor, who, in a manner similar to his colleague in Safe Space's municipality, endorsed historically entrenched notions of "the family" and rigid gender roles based on women's submission within it. He and his administration did not endorse the feminist, gender-equality perspective upon which Family Care had been founded a decade earlier. Family Care remained open; however, the strongly feminist founding director and a large majority of the staff resigned and were replaced with a new director and staff. The turnover, I heard from some of the remaining staff at Family Care and others, was related to the fundamental ideological differences between the mayor's perspective and feminists' perspectives on gender equality and relationships between men and women.

During 2002 and 2003, while I was engaged in various participant-observation activities at Family Care, their energies were largely focused on public family violence prevention campaigns, as per the new family-oriented demands of the municipal government. In November

2002, the staff initiated a monthlong "Good Treatment" violence prevention campaign. The campaign encouraged people to "treat each other well" by saying and doing nice things for one another in a variety of social contexts. It was devoid of any reference to the feminist tenets that had undergirded the origins of the focus on domestic violence in Chile. The cartoon figures in the campaign poster were mostly men in business suits, and the only females depicted were girls. The staff's choice of images for this campaign reflected Family Care's shift in focus from 1991, when they were founded, to 2002, when this campaign was launched. The Good Treatment campaign reflected a shift away from a gendered perspective to a rather more innocuous agenda of fomenting good treatment in all sorts of relationships within the society. This and other prevention campaigns that took place while I conducted my ethnographic work at Family Care drew much media attention to the mayor.

I observed how the paradigm of "Good Treatment" became a moral system through which the social actors on the staff could legitimately mobilize critiques and make demands about their needs as professionals and individuals. At one staff meeting, two of the therapists who worked directly with women who had suffered domestic violence were in charge of the self-care activities. They decided to mobilize the accepted, moralizing discourse around self-care in order to discuss an uncomfortable and underlying point of contention—the municipality's demand that they spend a certain part of their time on public prevention campaigns, like the Good Treatment campaign. The therapists who worked with women who suffered domestic violence felt that the time and energy the municipality demanded they spend on public campaigns left them exhausted and frustrated because it meant less time for them to interact with women who suffered. Each of these therapists worked only part-time at Family Care, twenty-two hours a week. A long waiting list of women who needed therapeutic care constantly faced them, and they knew they could not offer care to all of the women who needed it. The time demanded by the twice-yearly public prevention campaigns only worsened their possibilities to offer care for women who suffered gender-based violence.

Throughout that conversation the atmosphere in the staff meeting was tense. Family Care staff members were frustrated, and many expressed feeling like their agenda as an institution had been undermined and hijacked by the municipality's emphasis on high-profile, politically motivated prevention campaigns. One of the therapists who worked with women pointed out that as a staff they needed to stop fearing that the municipality could close Family Care. She posited that this fear was driving the prevention-centered focus of their work, as the prevention focus came from municipal officials. Someone else voiced a related frustration, noting that they often lacked even the most basic office resources to function effectively. They had only one computer, the printer and copier often did not function properly, and they frequently lacked basic office supplies such as printer paper. The lack of material resources necessary to achieve their institutional and personal work goals made all of their tasks even more taxing, time consuming, and frustrating.

Several staff members voiced their frustration that the demands on them were so great that they were not able to perform their duties adequately. They felt that often they were just going through the motions and were concerned that they were doing a lot of activities but doing nothing well or in-depth. One therapist noted that she really enjoyed doing prevention work, but, because of her frustrations with not having the resources to do a good job, she had less of a desire to work on prevention. Someone else noted that they needed to redefine their goals, given these resource limitations. Adding to the precariousness of the situation, most of the staff had neither full-time contracts nor the accompanying benefits, and therefore they lacked the job security that could have given them more freedom to pursue the work they deemed most necessary rather than focusing so heavily on high-profile prevention activities. The director noted that the staff, their material resources, and the overall budget had been greatly reduced. Although she expressed concern, she maintained that each staff member had to spend a certain amount of time on prevention each week. This was not negotiable. The mayor had decreed it.

As I approached the Family Care building during a brief visit in 2009, I noted new graffiti all over the now-dilapidated building, declaring, for example, "No to Capitalism." I soon learned, during my conversation with the new director, that the external, superficial dilapidation of the building that housed Family Care was symbolic of the deterioration of their programs for women who suffered intimate partner violence. She explained to me that the terrain had continued to rapidly change since I did my research in 2002 and 2003, with Family Care forced to adapt constantly to shifting political tides. By 2009, Family Care no longer had any sort of gender-inequality perspective on domestic violence. Their perspective was now fully focused on the couple, addressing relationships between the man and the woman. The former mayor of Safe Space's municipality, who had stormed out of the public hearing some years earlier and removed funding for their domestic violence program, was now mayor of Family Care's municipality, and his plan was to change Family Care dramatically, into an all-purpose family treatment center similar to the one in his former municipality. Family Care's director told me that this meant that they would offer various services to various family members, not only related to domestic violence. Probably they would be required to focus on older adults, she said, because older adults vote. She noted that the mayor was very interested in using Family Care campaigns to target voters. I raised the idea that public campaigns, such as Family Care's "Good Treatment" campaign in 2003, achieved the same thing. She agreed, with no hesitation. I was surprised by the straightforward nature of her critiques of the municipal administration under which she worked. In 2009, the director's perspective on the history of Family Care's shift confirmed my own observations from years earlier. Starting around 2001 when the feminists who had founded the center left, she said, the program began to deteriorate. When the director who was running the center when I did my research left, the situation worsened, as the new mayor did not prioritize the center.

Indeed, during a brief visit I made in 2006 to Family Care, staff members had expressed their concern that instead of having so many clients they needed a waiting list, as had been the case in 2003, they were often at loose ends, without clients. The director in 2009 told me that the community and society in general began to have a bad impression of Family Care and therefore women had stopped seeking help there. Staff left, and then no replacements were hired. She felt that SERNAM, with the increase in regional centers and shelters, was built up while Family Care was left fallow. I heard from a number of sources in 2009, however, that the regional SERNAM centers and shelters were not working well for women (see discussion of SERNAM below). By 2011 when I next visited Santiago, Family Care no longer existed as a center dedicated to women who had suffered domestic violence, just as the director had predicted when I spoke with her in 2009.

Throughout their history, Family Care's methodologies of care for women were contingent on broader political and economic tides. In particular, the municipal control of Family Care, like the funding Safe Space had received from their municipality, was tied to political will and disappeared when conservative mayors, associated with rigid gender roles emphasizing women's subordination, were elected. Care could not be continuous in such a context of insecurity. The deep changes feminists had envisioned and that had been enacted in Family Care's first decade, based implicitly on a feminist ethic of care, were constantly threatened by their appropriation by political forces whose ethics were much more firmly grounded in neoliberal moralities and rigid and historically entrenched gender roles based on women's inequality.

SERNAM's Care

In 2007, the Inter-American Commission on Women of the Organization of American States (OAS) released a report evaluating member states' implementation of the Convention of Belém do Pará (Beltrán-Martínez 2007). According to this report, Chile has done relatively well in most areas related to domestic violence services and laws, including the training of functionaries and the availability of shelters, which have been implemented throughout the country. Moreover, SERNAM has become firmly rooted as an institution of the state since its birth at the will of the feminist movement in 1991. The indicators of "global governance" (Merry 2011) had been fulfilled, but women who suffered gender-based violence in Chile faced the reality of collapsed care, and care largely based on ideologies different from those that had originally provided the basis for the institutionalization of gender-equality efforts and domestic violence programs.

As we talked in her downtown Santiago office during 2009, the final year of Michele Bachelet's presidency, a SERNAM official told me:

> I was militant in the women's movement during the dictatorship. That was my space where I fought during the dictatorship. . . . I think that the women's movement was the fundamental actor for the recuperation of democracy in Chile. It's painful for me to see how shrunken the women's movement is [now], the lack of resources, the lack of the movement's leadership.

She recognized that shelters constituted, in part, a Band-Aid measure to deal with inadequate judicial resources. She told me:

> The truth is that . . . for a long time we resisted the idea of governmental shelters. For one thing, because we posited, and I continue to believe it, that we should have a law that permits us to protect women more quickly, a quicker punishment for the aggressors, so that it is not women who have to be trapped, but he who has committed the crime. But as a country, we didn't have this . . . and some women were at risk. Because of that we made the decision to work with shelters.

This official recognized the inadequacies of the state's solutions to the problem of domestic violence. She expressed what I call a *pragmatic ethic of care*, which is exemplary of the state's policies, laws, and practices that have evolved around domestic violence against women in the twenty years since the state took on domestic violence as an object of surveillance.

By 2009, Ema at Safe Space was also critical of SERNAM's domestic violence programs, which had now spread throughout the country, telling me that in reality the shelters and systems were dysfunctional. The state, she implied, had learned nothing from its years of attention to domestic violence and left women woefully unprotected. The state was more interested in maintaining bureaucratic structures around domestic violence, not addressing women's gendered suffering and all of its complications and entanglements. A 2007 research report, led by Ximena Rojas Bravo at the nongovernmental organization DOMOS and Valentina Martínez, then at the nongovernmental feminist organization La Morada, and conducted at SERNAM's request, also pointedly criticized the Chilean state and SERNAM's continued lack of an integrated response to the problem of domestic violence. The report suggests that women need long-term companionship and a wide variety of resources and services as they travel their "critical route" (*Ruta Crítica*), conceived of as the complicated, winding, nonlinear pathways toward "recovery" from domestic violence (SERNAM et al. 2007). Ximena Rojas Bravo of DOMOS told me that SERNAM refused to publish this report in 2007 when it was completed, although SERNAM had requested and funded it, because the findings about the effectiveness of SERNAM's interventions were unfavorable (personal communication 2009). SERNAM finally published it, though only online, in 2009, two years after the study's completion. What the report found was consistent with the expression of what I call a pragmatic ethic of care by a SERNAM official I interviewed in 2009. A pragmatic ethic of care allows the state to provide only the most basic resources to women, not the kinds of long-term care the report suggests are necessary. Some intimated to me that the report's critique of this pragmatic ethic of care led to SERNAM's hesitance to publish it. One of the public prosecutors I interviewed in 2009 also emphasized the need for an integrated state-level response—in addition to the criminal response—to the varied needs of women who suffer domestic violence. "Domestic violence is about the negation of the person's use of their rights as a person," she asserted. But also it is an issue that demands care in the form of services and support for women, services and support that go well beyond the powers of the judicial system.

SERNAM's Shifting Gendered Ideologies

The contingent meanings of SERNAM's work can also be seen in the shifting nature of SERNAM's public campaigns around domestic violence. Since 1991 SERNAM has launched numerous public campaigns aimed at preventing and raising awareness about domestic violence. One such campaign in 2001 highlighted psychological violence as a form of violence, emphasizing that domestic violence not only encompasses physical violence but verbal abuse as well. Posters in this campaign, such as the one in Figure 6, sought to raise awareness about emotional and verbal abuse, urging, "Don't let violence destroy your intimate partnership" and proclaiming, "There are words that hurt. Control your words." Dripping from the nose of the woman in the poster are the painful words: "Whore, stupid, shut up, loose, useless, bitch," evoking a bloody stream. Similar posters ran on the sides of buses and in various venues in Santiago.

Figure 6. This campaign, "Don't let violence beat your partner/partnership" ("*No dejes que la violencia golpeé a tu pareja*"), encouraged youth to "realize that tolerance, respect, nondiscrimination, and acceptance of diversity are values that sustain real democracies," and aimed "to decrease the indices of violence and significantly improve male and female Chileans' quality of life."

Domestic violence campaigns have been framed as part of Chile's struggle to regain a fully democratic government and society. However, the bases of these campaigns fluctuate with political leadership. The most recent campaign, launched in 2010 under President Piñera's leadership, focused on feminizing men who abuse their female partners by calling them "faggots" (*maricones*) (see Figure 7a and 7b).

In this campaign the state showed itself to be homophobic and sexist, discarding the nuanced gender analysis that had underpinned SERNAM's work on domestic violence since its origin in 1991. The focus on violent men as "faggots" suggests that men should still enact a version of *machismo*, but one based on benevolent sexism (see Glick et al. 2000); in this model men are still in charge, protecting women as the supposedly, inherently weaker "second sex" (Beauvoir 1965). SERNAM's vision of gender under President Piñera is much closer to the women's gender roles promoted under Pinochet and historically in Chile: women as divine mothers, nurturers, and objects of men's desires, not protagonists of their own desires.

In another example of the state's promotion of a rigid femininity, based in part on objectification of women, in May 2011 SERNAM released a document to encourage women's participation in the labor market (SERNAM 2011). The manual begins with instructions for a woman to ready herself to successfully apply for remunerated work outside her home: how to clean her nails, wash her hair, and apply lotion and makeup. "The development of a personal brand is indispensable to achieve security in oneself and feeling attractive with how you are," the document proclaims. According to SERNAM under President Piñera, for a woman to prepare herself to participate in the labor market is to create a "personal brand" through particular attention to hairstyle, makeup, and clothing. In one exercise promoted by the "new" SERNAM, women are to reflect on "self-knowledge" questions such as: "Mirror, mirror, should I highlight or hide my waist?" This is reminiscent of the state's enforcement of gendered forms of embodiment during the dictatorship, when men were not to have long hair and women were not to wear pants. SERNAM's release of this document was heavily criticized by feminists, including the Observatorio Género y Equidad (Gender and Equity Observatory), because of a blatant lack

Figure 7a and 7b. In the posters and television spots famous male actors, sports figures, and artists declared with force: "A man who abuses a woman is a faggot. Let's use the word for the one who deserves it."

of sensitivity to the ways in which a focus on women's hair color and makeup reinforces stereotypical ideals of femininity without providing a critical gender perspective or fostering the development of actual work skills.[3] This is a reflection of the ways that SERNAM's agendas are contingent on shifting political leadership and the ideologies of gender and family under different political regimes, even though SERNAM was created with the mission of maintaining a critical gender analysis and promoting women's equality in society and labor markets.

Conclusions

From 2000 to 2010, Safe Space, Family Care, and SERNAM's programs were subject to shifting political terrains. Political struggles for adequate resources to address the myriad problems women who suffer domestic violence face were ongoing, and each center dealt with these challenges in different ways. In the early 2000s, Family Care was affected by the election of a conservative mayor that forced a shift from a feminist analysis to one in which domestic violence was addressed as protection for the family and women's traditional gender roles within families. Similarly, under President Piñera SERNAM has become heavily focused on the family and on promoting the aforementioned gender roles. On the other hand, Safe Space, an NGO, maintained a critical gender analysis of domestic violence in terms of women's inequality, but it also faced grave challenges to its ability to provide continuous care for women. In sum, each of these institutions has been beholden, in different ways, to the changing political and economic projects of municipal and national governments, as well as international agencies and funders. Their care has consistently been contingent, not continuous.

To differing extents, although Safe Space and Family Care did the work of bringing the state's ethic of gender equality and care for women who suffer domestic violence into practice, their programs, and the thrust of those programs, were contingent on resource distribution in the public sector and political will and leadership at interlinked local, national, and global levels. The conservative, center-right and right-wing coalition Alianza por Chile (Alliance for Chile) has shown itself to be deeply committed to fixed notions of women's acceptable gender roles, wherein femininity should revolve around a woman's self-abnegation and her devotion to her family. In this formulation, which denies the centrality of a gender-inequality paradigm for understanding domestic violence against women, the unity of the heterosexual nuclear family is the goal. It is women's role to maintain that unity, and the government must promote this kind of family for the "good of the nation."

Although SERNAM began as a firmly feminist institution of the state, based on a gendered perspective and the goal of gender equity, by the end of the first decade of the twenty-first century the contingencies of this institution's goals were palpable. As SERNAM has evolved and especially as it has operated under the leadership of the Alianza por Chile, its work with women who suffer gender-based violence has been increasingly critiqued by feminists and feminist organizations that work on behalf of or directly with women who have suffered gendered violence. Instead of being based on a feminist ethic of care, SERNAM's goals have increasingly been based on the bureaucratic and neoliberal goals associated with Chile's appearance as a modern, developed country.

Similarly, Bumiller (2008) contends that the original feminist analysis around sexual violence in the United States has been diluted and that sexual violence against women has largely become depoliticized and is no longer discussed and addressed as a gender-equality issue. She contends that this depoliticization has come about in the United States as the issue has been brought (or at times forced) into the realm of the state and institutionalized, to be dealt with by the "therapeutic state" with its "network of professionals, social workers, and government agents providing service delivery to the poor and disadvantaged" (p. xii).

At Family Care, the shift in political leadership meant the channeling of more funds to their programs to prevent intimate violence, producing high-profile publicity for the mayor of the municipality. This resulted in fewer resources for women who sought help there. Safe Space was forced to close down its treatment program for some years after the municipality cut funding for the program there. Due to links with international organizations and the international community working to combat violence against women, Safe Space was able to dedicate its energies to other projects—both national and regional in nature. Safe Space maintained its independence from the state—an intentional stance produced from the recognition of the importance of NGOs as monitors of the state in the arena of gender equity and violence against women. Several women's rights NGOs in Chile have been involved in these efforts, including DOMOS, La Morada, and Humanas.

CHAPTER 7

The Ills of Medicalizing Violence and the Work of Ethnography in Processes of Care

Care . . . is work as well as an emotion or motive
or intention. —Virginia Held (2006:51)

The Ills of Medicalizing Violence

A violent and catastrophic "event" does not have to happen all at once. The violent event can be a sum total of everyday forms of violence that congeal over time. For Luz, Marisol, and Josefina various forms of everyday violence coalesced to become the event that produced the poisonous knowledge that they continuously worked through. Conceptualizing the everydayness of violence as the event for Luz, Marisol, and Josefina points to the importance of developing and practicing an ethic of care that prioritizes curing, addressing, and fixing the various forms of seemingly mundane, banal violence that are entangled and interconstructed with gender-based intimate partner violence against women. Concomitantly, caring for women who have already experienced traumatic violence emerges as crucial. By illuminating and analyzing the experiences of Luz, Marisol, and Josefina, *Traumatic States* constitutes an act of witnessing poisonous violence and an argument for more effective forms of care for women—care that is both prior to and following the event of domestic violence.

The stories of Josefina, Marisol, and Luz continue into the present. Their suffering has been extraordinary in severity and in terms of what it has done to their lives and experiences of being in the world, and this suffering folds into the ordinary in ways that are both perceptible and imperceptible, even as historical contingencies at local, state, and global scales shift in favor of women's rights.

159

Instead of interventions such as meaningful job training or new living arrangements, Josefina, Luz, and Marisol were prescribed psychoactive medications by state and local government agencies in order to address depressive symptoms related to the abuses they suffered throughout their lives. Each woman dealt with her difficulties in her own ways and had different resources from which to draw; their "recoveries" depended largely on their individual activities in help-seeking and their histories in relationship to the state and ideas about their rights. Luz eventually fared well in the sense that she had the opportunity to work in a meaningful job, which paid well and provided health care for her. She seemed to draw from her "rebellious streak" in seeking out spiritual pathways that helped her to recuperate her sense of self. But, also, her abusive husband had killed himself right after he tried to murder her, and so he was gone, never to return. Marisol also had a strong educational background and sense of her rights as a person, which she continually mobilized in order to seek what she needed. Her financial situation was tenuous, and by 2009 she could not work for remuneration due to her myriad health problems. Her work consisted instead of seeking reparations from her abusive husband and from the state. Josefina still lived with her abusive husband and struggled with chronic depression due to the lifetime of gender-based violence she suffered. She felt she lacked viable options for making her own way in the world and saw no possibilities for the future other than her continued dependence on a variety of psychoactive medications and continual search for support from the government.

Luz, Marisol, and Josefina are not self-contained, completely self-regulated, and self-determined individuals, composed of "mind" on the one hand and "body" on the other. However, systems of care often treat them as such and work to medicalize their suffering by treating symptoms and failing to address the etiology of that suffering within social, political, and economic bodies. Care for individuals is crucial, but that is only one facet of treatment based in an ethic of care.

In one illustrative instance, Josefina described how she suffered rape by her husband as a deep violation of both her bodily *and* psychological integrity—a wound that would never be healed. In those violent episodes her husband asserted that he, in that moment and whenever he wanted, in a sense owned her body and her mind. Novel state policies, nongovernmental organizations, and grassroots women's rights groups have the potential to disrupt this ideology of men's ownership of women's bodies. Instead, these groups assert, women are entitled to ownership over their own bodies, minds, and lives. The health effects of violence against women—defined in terms of the overall well-being of a person, the mindful body, and the embodied mind—are clear in statistical and global analyses and in the fine-grained ethnographic detail about Marisol's, Luz's, and Josefina's lives and circumstances. A state of health includes freedom from gender violence, which is a social, not individual, biomedical problem. Josefina, Marisol, and Luz assert the need for a panoply of resources from which to select.

The Ills of Prioritizing Juridical Surveillance

The state's moves toward medicalization of violence via psychotherapeutic, biomedical, and pharmaceutical interventions have dovetailed with the state's heavy investment in bureaucracies and mechanisms of the judicial system. Since 1990 the Chilean state's gaze has been fixed on domestic violence as part of its project to "modernize" the judicial system. Sentences for domestic violence have become increasingly harsh, state centers for women have proliferated, awareness of domestic violence has increased, and femicide has been typified as a crime. Women are now considered full, adult citizens, with codified rights to live a life free from intimate forms of violence. Just as the state's violence perpetrated during the dictatorship is now interrogated and some offenders jailed, men's intimate violence against women, while still rampant, is deemed officially unacceptable by the state and punishable by law. More than ninety safe houses are available to women who seek shelter from abusive husbands. Family courts, lawyers, psychologists, and social workers, paid by the state, are available. These innovations would seem to point to a state in which women's citizenship in the intertwined spheres of society and home has become fully realized. But Josefina, Luz, and Marisol speak to show otherwise.

Josefina, Luz, and Marisol live complicated lives; the etiologies of their suffering in domestic violence are social, political, economic, and cultural. The solutions offered by the state are usually bureaucratic and channeled through the judicial system. Marisol's detailed narrative of weaving in and out of juridical and medical systems over the course of a decade points to the heavily bureaucratic nature of care for women who suffer intimate violence. The state's gaze on domestic violence has led to its substantial investment in judicial mechanisms, in particular, in the form of courts, court officials, social workers, and psychologists to certify and validate women's suffering. The state's dedication of resources to punitive structures ensures that when women—often women with few socioeconomic resources—report their abusive partners to the state, the state's interventions reinforce the already persistent inequalities within the wider society. Resources dedicated to the judicial system emphasize the punishment of domestic violence offenders instead of the improvement of care for those, like Marisol, Luz, and Josefina, who suffer from that violence.

The dedication of resources to and focus on the judicial system allows the state to consolidate its power through a sort of humanitarian surveillance, a novel form of biopower that links intimate spheres with social inequalities through the disciplinary spaces of the judicial system, which are in turn entwined with biomedical and psychological interventions. Forms of care not legitimized by the state exist, but they are highly contingent and in a state of disrepair. They must be constantly and consciously maintained through sustained activism. This, despite the fact that Josefina, Marisol, and Luz needed and desired interventions outside of the juridico-medical systems. The state's interventions, which only offer some forms of care, are deemed less dispensable than the nonmedical and nonjuridical interventions offered by Safe Space and Family Care, which are constantly at risk. The knowledge that agencies and women themselves have about domestic violence and the care required to intervene in abusive relationships is implicitly deemed less valuable than the technical knowledge produced in the state's systems. What counts as knowledge and which knowledge has the power to shift resources matters to the lives of women like Luz, Marisol, and Josefina.

Legal reforms and innovations are crucial for addressing violence against women. However, the law only provides a set of rules for behavior and consequences for noncompliance. Only behavior that is deemed to be a violation of the law can be addressed by the legal system. The judicial arm of the state is extremely capable of assessing right and wrong and punishing wrong behavior, but ethics are both prior to and after the law. How might an ethic of care fill in the gaps of the bureaucratic forms of care offered by the state via the judicial system? An ethic of care for women who have suffered domestic violence emerges as a crucial foundation for the interventions and programs to support and nurture women's recoveries. Relationships based on a professional ethic of care are not disposable. Care is work and process. Family Care, Safe Space, and SERNAM's programs have at times been based on such an ethic of care, which can be implemented and maintained by the state, just as judicial and biomedical interventions are institutionalized.

Ethics of Care: Recovering Meaning

Luz, Marisol, and Josefina drew on bureaucratic, legal, and medical forms of care. However, their needs extend well beyond what those forms of care could provide; they need flexible, creative care to address the particular constellations of violence they suffer. Domestic violence presents particularly novel challenges to state interventions, and the women's narratives give voice to some of the special dangers involved when the institutional structures and bureaucracies built up around the state's interventions become rigid, static, and unresponsive to women's real life needs.

An ethic of care demands that limited resources be redirected. Dedicating resources to judicial and medical interventions to the detriment of other interventions needed by women who suffer domestic violence fails to recognize that the struggle is often about more than getting free from violence. It is also about constructing, creating, imagining, and recreating a meaningful life in relationship to others. Marisol, Luz, and Josefina are driven not simply to be free from violence but to live meaningful lives. Often these desires are contingent on the kinds of opportunities that exist. They, along with other women, voiced their desires to be free from violence but also to have opportunities for meaningful work; for developing their interests beyond being a wife, housewife, mother, and victim; for economic independence; and for adequate access to health and dental care. However, newly "regendered" programs, policies, and ideologies of the state often do not engage fully with these desires. Instead, Josefina, Luz, and Marisol often confronted barriers within systems of care. Nevertheless, Marisol and Luz, in particular, were able to use those systems in order to construct meaning.

Gendered Citizenship

Josefina, Luz, and Marisol inhabit very different life circumstances, yet they share deep similarities. They all critique inadequate state resources for the problem of intimate partner violence, which illuminates a damaging slippage between the Chilean state's claims to gender equality and modernity (cf. Lazarus-Black 2007; Plesset 2006), on the one hand, and the state's failure to provide full membership for them as citizens, on the other. Each of these three women inhabits very different family, educational, and political life circumstances. But they are inextricably linked together by a form of gendered citizenship. Marisol's narrative shows particularly vividly how she again and again had to actively make herself into a citizen-subject legible to the state, her gendered citizenship revolving around the enactment of her gendered role as a victim of domestic violence. This notion of personal responsibility for fixing oneself, bettering oneself, *making and proving oneself worthy* lies at the crux of the neoliberal ideology about citizenship (Merry 2006; Ong 2006). Those who cannot achieve this level of self-efficacy to seek and demand help from the state and behave "properly" while doing so are cast out or socially abandoned (Biehl 2005). In effect, this is a moral system wherein only certain kinds of certifiable "victims" are able to access justice, or some modified version thereof. In the case of domestic violence, the majority of sufferers are female, which thus implies a form of gendered citizenship that only certain women can access, and to differing degrees.

Marisol, Josefina, and Luz are bound together by the realities that they mutually critique. Some mechanisms provided by the state are helpful, but in all three women's cases, judicial and biomedical interventions proved to be less than adequate; resources for the creation of new paths to personhood and social engagement are severely limited. Reparations for the state's lack of attention to violence against women, and therefore the state's complicity with this form of violence, are not forthcoming in the myriad ways Luz, Marisol, and Josefina have expressed needing.

Women's experiences of intimate partner violence and the state's inadequate responses to them truncate women's rights as full citizens, showing a gendered form of what Caldeira and Holston (1999:692) have termed "disjunctive citizenship," wherein "the development of citizenship is never cumulative, linear, or evenly distributed for all citizens, but is always a mix of progressive and regressive elements, uneven, unbalanced and heterogeneous." In intimate partner violence, state and family meet to control and constrain women's agency in particular ways, in particular circumstances, and with emotional effects (Das 1995). When governments do not provide the tools and resources required for full citizenship and gender equality, even when they claim to do so, perpetrators experience impunity from the state and the society (cf. Gill 2004; Green 1999).

The inadequacy of state resources, along with the resulting inability of women to obtain adequate help, contributes to maintaining violent relationships, often giving women little room to imagine and rework their lives outside of the violence. Fear, "the memory of pain" as Allan Young (1997) describes it, conditions the memory and acts to constrain agency in specifically gendered ways. In many cases, the inadequacies of state policies and practices produce memories of pain both in the intimate relationship and in help-seeking endeavors. In these ways, state and affect are intertwined (see also Jenkins 1991; DelVecchio Good and Good 1988). Instead of making major structural changes that would put the burden on the state to guarantee equal citizenship, the state compels women who suffer intimate partner violence to activate services and resources. It is women's work to make themselves full citizens in the face of intimate partner violence.

The Work of Ethnography in Processes of Care

When Josefina, Luz, and Marisol first sought care, bureaucracies intervening in domestic violence had only existed in Chile for about a decade. These bureaucracies were based on novel models of intervention for a newly visible problem, models that quickly became the new "norm" for care, whether or not they were actually beneficial to women in the long term. Once bureaucratized, forms of care can become entrenched as the new "normal." They become the newest version of "the way things are," making it difficult to shift policies and practices as new knowledge emerges and needs change. The normalization of bureaucratic processes that are harmful produces a gap between the state's claims to provide care for women who suffer domestic violence and the state's practices, which fail to provide that care.

The ongoing production of ethnographic knowledge about the ways that bureaucracies intertwine with affective experiences could be part of a new, nontechnological *process of care* capable of addressing the constantly shifting social, political, and economic landscapes that women must navigate to seek help and engage in recovery. Just as bio-technological innovation is dependent on finely tuned empirical data and constant research and development, an ethnographically informed process of care entails careful ethnographic exploration of women's lives and dialogue with those who have the power to shift resources and discourses. Adequate provision of care requires addressing the entangled roots of various forms of violence. Experience-near ethnography can enable such ongoing, always developing, and changing processes of care. Ethnography in conversation with bureaucratic practices can help avoid the normalization of violence that can take root in and be perpetuated by bureaucracies that fail to be self-critical. Ethnography can illuminate the complicated effects of state policies and bureaucracies and reveal how structures that are rigid and unable to ascertain and engage in meaningful readjustments are at risk of becoming purveyors of normalized violence and thereby perpetuating domestic violence against women. Ethnography can provide a remedy to structures that purport to provide care but that do not.

Ethnographic research privileges experiential knowledge and allows for the production of anthropological knowledge about the gendered contexts of distress, suffering, and recoveries within ongoing contexts of inequality (cf. Guarnaccia, Lewis-Fernández, and Rivera Marano 2003). More specifically, it is crucial not only to examine individual women's processes of recovery from domestic violence, but also to examine those processes in terms of their interactions with various contexts. Creating and perpetuating new bureaucratic structures in the absence of empirical knowledge of the ways in which such structures affect real women's lives constitutes a form of normalized violence insofar as women experience harm because of it. Ethnography's power to contribute nuanced understandings of how bureaucracies produce harmful effects can be employed by those in public health and political leadership to reorient bureaucratic practices toward more adaptable and therefore more effective interventions. In sum, the production of ethnographic knowledge is crucial to the continual process of defining and redefining an ethic of care positioned to undermine gendered violence and its effects.

Coda: Addressing Pre-Traumatic Stress, Not Only Post-Traumatic Stress

Instead of addressing the health effects of the violence only *after the fact*, once it has been inflicted, once it has caused the *post*-traumatic stress, the testimonies of Marisol, Josefina, and Luz attest to the need to unwind and address the inequalities, the forms of structural violence, that are interconstructed in gendered ways with domestic violence against women within particular local contexts (Merry 2009). These inequalities are "historically given."[1] That is, they are related to historical processes of subjugation, processes that have benefited some while leaving others lacking. In order to address the suffering that stems from domestic violence, it is necessary to cure the inequalities that provide the conditions of possibility for such violence to flourish. Some of these inequalities are local and others are national or global. Understanding and curing the inequalities that produce and reproduce damaging forms of gender violence against women is critical for women's health.

APPENDIX I

Life History Interviews

The life history narrative was the primary form of data collection I employed to answer research questions. Life history narratives are crucial for gathering data about how women's experiences of health and illness are related to social, political, economic, and cultural contexts and women's particular situations within these contexts. These data, drawn from women with various situations and treatment outcomes, provide rich detail about women's experiences of domestic violence and recovery. The life history interview, a form of unstructured interviewing (Bernard 1995), is an important way to understand how larger historical forces and political-economic structures affect people's lives in specific ways (Mintz 1960) and women's lives in particular (Behar and Gordon 1995; Personal Narratives Group 1989). Life history narratives are also used in therapeutic contexts in Chile for women who have suffered domestic violence (Padín 2001), illustrating its cultural congruence with the research population (Renzetti, Edleson, and Kennedy Bergen 2001).

The life history interview is an especially important tool for research on women's experiences, as women's experiences are often absent in historical renderings and their voices are left unheard. With the life history interview, women's experiences are brought to the forefront and can later be analyzed in terms of the historical contexts surrounding and informing them. Such an approach is important in reconstructing the past through individuals' narratives, especially narratives by those disenfranchised by dominant regimes, power structures, and institutions. For women who suffered domestic violence, whose possibilities to exert their wills are co-opted within their most intimate spheres and by structural violence embedded in the justice system, it is indispensable.

The life history interview is also a relatively noninvasive way to investigate very sensitive and personal experiences. In my research I viewed the life history interview as a process in which building trust with the interviewee was of paramount importance. During the first interview with each woman, I invited her to tell me about her life, starting with whatever aspect of her life she wished to share first. Some women wanted a more specific question, to which I responded by asking questions such as "Where did you grow up?" and then using noninvasive follow-up questions to ease them into the process. The idea behind beginning the interview process in this way was that each woman would feel as comfortable as possible in narrating her experience. It is important in such research (as with research on torture by the state, for example) that the interviewee be adequately supported in the information collection process, that she be potentially able to use the interview as an opportunity to assign meaning to her life and its events, and that every effort is made to have the experience be empowering. In other words, it is essential to avoid making the experience one in which the victim is revictimized; instead, the researcher's goal should be to do the opposite. These of course are ideals and do not always come to fruition, but it is ethically imperative that the researcher be consciously aware of these goals and respect the human rights of the interviewee in every way possible.

I used this method of data collection because it provided data related to the contexts of women's experiences of domestic violence, help-seeking, and recovery from *their* points of view. The goal was to understand how each woman framed her life experiences in general and these life experiences in particular. In this way it was possible to investigate the meanings women assigned to life events and to solicit information noninvasively about their feelings and emotions related to domestic violence, as well as the complicated contexts of these experiences.

The interview process for each woman depended on her own style of relating her life history and her level of engagement with the interview. I attempted to gauge, based on each woman's reactions and responses, when it would be appropriate to ask more specific questions designed to provide data about particular research concerns. I attempted to elicit from each informant two "histories." First, I sought each woman's general life history and the political, historical, and personal contexts surrounding her experiences of domestic violence and recovery. Second, I tried to elicit her illness history, a medical anthropological method (Kleinman 1988) that includes her understanding of her history of domestic violence and trauma, in order to investigate the mental and physical illness experiences (Kleinman 1995) related to domestic violence and to situate such experiences within her broader personal life history.

The following represent a small sample of key questions I posed to elicit this information:

1. BASIC PROBING QUESTIONS: What have been the most important events in your life? What was your life like during the military regime? (Probes included questions, for example, about political involvement, education, jobs, family, friends, and romantic relationships.)

2. MAIN QUESTION: Did you ever try to escape from domestic violence during the dictatorship? FOLLOW-UP QUESTIONS: If so, why did you do so at that time, and from whom did you seek help? Did this intervention work, in your estimation? If you did not seek help, can you identify what factors prevented you from doing so? How is your life different now than it was when you were experiencing domestic violence during the dictatorship?

3. MAIN QUESTION: Describe your attempts to seek help during the postdictatorship era. FOLLOW-UP QUESTIONS: How did you decide to seek help? Where did you go? How did you arrive at this center? How has the treatment at this center affected your life situation?[1]

4. MAIN QUESTION: What do you define as "recovery"? FOLLOW-UP QUESTION: Based on your own concept, do you feel that you have recovered?

5. MAIN QUESTION: Tell me about any health problems you've had and treatments you've sought for these problems, since

you began experiencing domestic violence. FOLLOW-UP
QUESTIONS: Do you attribute these health problems to
any particular life experience or situation? Have you sought
professional medical care for this condition or these conditions?
If so, whom have you consulted and for what reasons? Was the
treatment adequate? Describe.

In the interview process with women who suffered domestic violence, I spent the first interview building each woman's confidence,
getting to know her and her comfort level, and gauging her willingness and capability to continue. For each interview following the first,
I went over the data collected during the previous interview in order to
maximize each interview session (cf. Lincoln and Guba 1985). Then
I analyzed how best to progress in the interview to highlight specific
instances and understand important details of her life, health problems, experiences in the judicial and health care systems, and current
situation.

It is important to note that the women I interviewed all had sought
help for problems of domestic violence. Therefore, they constitute a
special population. In addition, many of them still lived in relationships of varying degrees of violence at the time of the interviews, while
many others were completely separated from the abuser.

APPENDIX 2

Table 1. Forms of Violence Reported

	Santiago	Santiago	Araucania Region	Family Care	Safe Space	Parson's Research
	1994[1]	2002[2]	2002[3]	1997[4]	2002[5]	2003
Some form of partner violence	60%	50%	50%	100%	100%	100%
Physical violence	26%	32%	25%	54%	68%	83%
Sexual violence	26%	14%	14%	33%	37%	33%
Economic violence	n/a	n/a	n/a	57%	46%	56%
Psychological violence	34%	43%	43%	100%	95%	100%

Note that the first three columns are data from population-level research, the fourth and fifth columns are drawn from Safe Space and Family Care client populations, and the final column is drawn from my own research sample. Therefore, these data are not comparable in terms of methodologies, but they do illustrate that, at each of these levels, rates are fairly similar.

1. These data are from the first population-level study of intimate partner violence in Chile. The figures presented here specifically cover Santiago (see Larraín 1994).
2. These data are from a population-level study conducted by SERNAM in 2001 in Santiago (see SERNAM 2002).
3. These figures specifically cover the Araucania Region, which is a more rural region of Chile, and are drawn from the same population-level study conducted by SERNAM in 2001, cited above (see SERNAM 2002).
4. These data derive from a Family Care study of their client population (personal communication 2003).
5. These data emerged from a Safe Space study of their client population (personal communication 2003).

Table 2. Data on Key Populations

	Family Care 1997	Safe Space 2002	Parson's Research 2003
Participants	3,000	1,012	18
Age range	21–50 (88%)[1]	21–50 (90%)	28–51 (100%)
Married	85%	82%	82%
Have not completed high school	56%	56%	—
Occupation—housework	43%	50%	50%
Wage labor	48%	29%	50%
Anxiety	—	79%	100%
Anxiety/depression[2]	21%	—	—
Depression	—	73%	100%
Physical health issues	—	77%	61%
Case in judicial system	42%	30%	39%

1. All percentages indicate the percent of the total sample for the particular study being reported. This means that the percentages do not always add up to 100 percent for each category.
2. The only data about anxiety and depression that exist for Family Care's client population combines anxiety and depression.

Notes

Prologue

1. More specifically, 33.9 percent reported that they had experienced psychological violence alone, and 25.9 percent had experienced both physical and psychological violence. Larraín's data showed that women reported more physical violence in the middle and lower classes than in the upper class and reported similar levels of psychological violence (Larraín 1994). Larraín (1994) argues that the low level of physical violence reported in the middle class and especially the upper classes reflects more the reticence of women in these classes to fully disclose their situations than an actual disparity in levels of physical violence.

2. In the 2002 study, 50.3 percent of women reported having lived some type of domestic violence, with 34 percent reporting physical and/or sexual violence (and, by implication, psychological violence), and 16.3 percent reporting psychological violence (SERNAM 2002:17, 19). Again in this study there were much higher levels of physical and/or sexual violence reported in lower classes (42.8%) than in middle and upper classes (26.7%), whereas levels of psychological violence were relatively similar across classes (SERNAM 2002:25).

3. In 2008, the first year that SERNAM, the Chilean National Women's Service, began registering such crimes on their website, fifty-nine women were murdered by male intimate partners, victims of the newly classified crime of femicide. In 2009, fifty-five women were murdered; in 2010, forty-nine women died; and, so far in 2011, thirteen cases have been classified as femicides.

Chapter I

1. Herman (1992) noted in her seminal work that experiences of captivity produced out of state violence and armed conflict, for instance, are more easily recognized as traumatic, whereas other situations of "captivity," like the family, have more often remained invisible. Herman argued: "Prolonged,

repeated trauma . . . occurs only in circumstances of captivity in prisons, concentration camps, and slave labor camps . . . and in families." Further, Herman argued: "political captivity is generally recognized, whereas the domestic captivity of women . . . is often unseen" (74).

2. Janis Jenkins has used this phrase in her work with survivors of political violence (Jenkins 1996).

3. Scarry theorizes: "The failure to express pain . . . will always work to allow its appropriation and conflation with debased forms of power; conversely, the successful expression of pain will always work to expose and make impossible that appropriation and conflation" (1985:14).

4. Biehl's *Vita: Life in a Zone of Social Abandonment,* an ethnographic exploration of Catarina's misdiagnosis, pharmaceuticalization, and gendered violence in Brazil, is exemplary of a critical phenomenological analysis in contemporary medical anthropology. Biehl (2005) and Das (2000) advocate focus on subjectivities in anthropological analyses.

5. The mindful body is made up of the body politic, the social body, and the individual body and points to the interrelations and interconstructions of mind, body, and society (Scheper-Hughes and Lock 1987).

6. Women who suffer their partners' violence are at risk for a range of mental and physical health issues, including depression, anxiety, gastrointestinal disorders, headaches, generalized aches and pains, and sexually transmitted diseases (Ceballo et al. 2004; Chen et al. 2009; Coker et al. 2002; Farmer 2005).

7. Common mental health effects include post-traumatic stress disorder (PTSD), other anxiety disorders, and major depressive disorder (Mechanic et al. 2008; Murthy 2001). A study on domestic violence and mental health in Chile, in particular, found that women who suffered domestic violence reported higher levels of depressive affect and post-traumatic stress disorder (Ceballo et al. 2004). In order to address such issues, and based on research on women's experiences in primary health care settings in Chile, Martínez (2009:96) has asserted that the Ministry of Health needs to create a health program that prioritizes freedom from violence as necessary for good health.

8. In Chile a law now defines murder of women by their intimates as femicide (*femicidio*).

9. Bumiller (2008:13) has critiqued how "it has become nearly impossible to understand the causes and consequences of being a victim of violence in terms which do not fit squarely within the purview of medicine or criminal justice." Health has also been critiqued as a normalizing moral framework (Metzl and Kirkland 2011).

10. On masculinities in Chile see Montecino and Acuña (1996), Olavarría (2001a, 2001b), Olavarría and Moletto (2002), and Quiroz (1991). It is also important to note that these images of Chilean women as self-abnegating mothers and reproducers of the household within the "private" sphere and

not as political actors are ideologies heavily employed by but not originating with Pinochet's regime (Jaquette 1989).

11. This number is officially documented in the "Chilean Truth and Reconciliation Commission Report," otherwise known as the Rettig Report (Comisión Chilena de Derechos Humanos and Fundación Ideas 1999; Rettig 1993).

12. I went to the memorial site of Villa Grimaldi with Luz and women's groups in honor of the thirtieth anniversary of the coup, which I describe in Chapter 3.

13. Chilean anthropologist Ximena Bunster-Burotto (1986:307) posits that torture of a woman was "consciously and systematically directed at her female sexual identity and female anatomy. . . . These [military-police were] not simply males 'out of control with permission' . . . the sexual torture of women [was] named 'control' and [was] authorized by state 'security.'"

14. See also Stern's trilogy *The Memory Box of Pinochet's Chile* (2004, 2006, 2010).

15. Loveman and Lira (2002) point out that the authoritarianism espoused and perpetrated by the dictatorship did not signify a total departure from tendencies already embedded in Chilean culture and society but were historically present. The use of state power under Pinochet was at the extreme end of the spectrum.

16. The dictatorial state used a network of mothers' centers (CEMAs) to promote rigid gender roles and ideologies as a gendered form of social control, especially in poorer areas. Mothers' centers were used to manipulate and deploy dominant gender ideologies as a particular point of power, and they illustrate the gendered nature of the dictatorship's authoritarianism. Through their deployment as ideological tools of the repressive regime, they were used to promote dominant gender roles—centering around "the images of the self-sacrificing patriotic housewife" and women's responsibilities as mothers, wives, and reproducers of family and nation—and to reinstate gendered class roles (Chuchryk 1989:138–39). Upper-class women's roles in the CEMAs consisted mostly of volunteering to "teach" lower-class women how to fulfill their roles as wives and mothers (Valdés 1991:98–101). Upper-class women's complicity with this project is notable and upholds Enloe's (1983:220) assertion that "military strategists need women. They need women who will act and think as patriarchy expects women to act and think." Indeed, as Hodgson (1995:121) notes, "patriarchies are rarely comprised of just men; it is in the interest, at times, of certain women or categories of women to collaborate with patriarchal projects." By 1983 there were as many as ten thousand CEMAs throughout Chile. Membership reached 230,000, including 6,000 volunteers (Chuchryk 1989:138).

17. Levinson (1989) similarly presented cross-cultural data confirming the existence of domestic violence in various locations throughout the world but also places where domestic violence did not occur.

18. Rich anthropological conversations on various regimes of "deservingness" surround access to care for undocumented migrants (see Chavez 2008; Willen 2011).
19. Autonomy therefore, Held explains, is relational; the individual responsibility that is core to the neoliberal political, economic, and moral regime is paradoxically based in social relationships and access to resources. The point is not to become a better neoliberal subject but to suggest that neoliberal morality is flawed and other moralities such as an ethic of care should be considered more thoroughly.
20. See Appendix 1 for more detailed explication of my methodological approaches.
21. Alvarez, Dagnino, and Escobar (1998) have identified that this is a danger more generally for Latin American feminist NGOs in relation to state governments.
22. They point to how "the analyst always needs to interpret such contextualization critically and to incorporate sources external to the narrative. Narrators of life stories, in other words, should be regarded as privileged but not definitive observers of their own historical contexts" (Maynes et al. 2008:45).
23. See Stacey (1988) and Wheatley (1994) for debates on intimacy between researcher and research participants in feminist ethnographic research.
24. My work is founded in and provides an ethnographic exploration of, in part, Elaine Scarry's (1985) influential work where she elaborates a theory that pain is a manifestation of absolute power and that pain destroys language.
25. Ticktin's recent work shows how care and damage are often linked (2011).
26. On suffering and possibilities for creativity, see Das and Kleinman (2001:19).

Chapter 2

1. This resonates with Merry's (2006) point that in various contexts when women recur to the judicial system in cases of domestic violence, "Women are choosing between two incompatible subject positions, one the rights-bearing subject, the other the good wife. Each represents a vision of the self that produces self-esteem, but the battered woman cannot simultaneously enact both. Choosing either one represents a failure of the other. The practices of the legal system are thus of critical significance to the woman's decision as she ambivalently moves in and out of this subjectivity" (186).
2. This "culture of reconciliation" takes place through the framework of "structural deflection," which other anthropologists have similarly described as "the diverted gaze of the state" (Scheper-Hughes 1992). Lazarus-Black (2007) broadens our view of how true equality for women is substituted by formal, legalized equality, which is exemplary of broader patterns as well as the more specific "politics of place" in Trinidad.

3. In her work on truth and reconciliation commissions in various countries throughout the world, including Chile, Hayner (2001:6) identified several key actions for bringing about reconciliation on a national level, including: "a clear end to the threat of further violence; a reparations program for those injured; attention to structural inequalities and basic material needs of victimized communities; the existence of natural linkages in society that bring formerly opposing parties together; or, most simply (although often overlooked) the simple passage of time." Though Hayner's focus is on national reconciliation, certain parallels can be drawn between the processes on individual and national levels, particularly in Chile. The steps she identifies as crucial to national reconciliation processes are clearly applicable to cases of domestic violence. The lack of attention to these steps was evident in women's narratives in 2004. Similarly, the state has continued to be the target of criticisms because of the lack of full attention to these aspects of reconciliation for victims of state terror during the era of the dictatorship (Gobierno de Chile 2005b).

4. Marisol shared with me a variety of what I label "official documents," which came from local and national government officials in judicial and therapeutic agencies, as well as from Safe Space.

5. It is important to remember that the women I interviewed who had these complaints about the judicial system shared several commonalities. They had all (1) sought help at either Family Care or Safe Space, where they accessed judicial assistance of some type; (2) filed a case in the judicial system; (3) followed up with their cases in the judicial system; and (4) chosen to share their stories with me.

Chapter 3

1. The online availability of this document in June 2010 through the Chilean National Library website is a sign of the state's move toward transparency during the postdictatorship era. Congressional representatives María Antonieta Saa and Adriana Muñoz, who had been leaders of the women's rights movement in the 1980s and were influential in the passage of the 1994 Family Violence Law, brought proposed changes to the 1994 Family Violence Law to congress in 1999. Their proposal was based on research findings of both strengths and weaknesses in the original law (Gobierno de Chile 2005a). The 1999 congressional proposal outlined various problems with the Family Violence Law of 1994 and its application, which included the following (this is a truncated list): lack of economic and human resources and well-prepared officials, inadequate training for judicial officials about family violence, inefficient application of the law, problematic emphasis on reconciliation (which happened in 65 to 70 percent of cases), insufficient restraining orders that

often go unenforced, ineffectiveness of therapy as a punishment, lack of follow-up, and lack of police protocol about how to deal with various kinds of family violence situations (Gobierno de Chile 2005a:6–8). Many of these complaints coincided with those voiced by women and professionals I interviewed during 2003 and 2004.

2. Many representatives also pointed to the importance of fomenting cultural changes, not only changes to the legal system, in order to confront family violence.

3. The advertisements, which employed "scientific" graphs and charts to argue that divorce has led to increases in domestic violence, as well as to drug and alcohol addiction for children of divorced parents in the United States and other countries, aired during the popular *telenovelas* (soap operas) on most Chilean television stations. Many governmental and nongovernmental figures and organizations came out strongly against this media campaign, arguing that their statistics constituted false knowledge. One article referred to this media blitz as a "campaign of terror" (Hidalgo 2003).

4. Article 74 stipulates that the mediator must ensure that both parties have equal opportunity and ability to make autonomous decisions and, lacking this, must find a way to provide for this "equilibrium" or end the mediation process. It specifies that "it is presumed that equality of conditions between the spouses does not exist if one of those has been the object of family violence by the other." Article 78 notes that the mediators specifically must not have committed family violence themselves (in addition to other crimes). The law also makes provisions for the economically most disadvantaged member (usually the woman). This inclusion of articles specifically addressing cases of family violence represents an achievement for congressional representatives interested in women's rights.

5. See Chapters 3 and 4 for discussion of the Family Treatment Center in this municipality as well as in the municipality where Family Care is located.

6. The default regime for property rights upon marriage used to be a conjugal society (*sociedad conyugal*), in which the husband had the determining rights over administration of the couple's property as well as rights over the legal representation of the wife. The couple could opt for a "separation of goods" (*separación de bienes*) instead, in which each person maintains ownership of her/his goods prior to and during the marriage. This, although not as glaringly patriarchal as the conjugal society regime, often (and this is the case with many of the women I interviewed) put women in a compromised position since women make less money than men for similar jobs and more often perform unremunerated work in the home (Fries and Matus 1999:115).

7. See "Tribunales de familia," Biblioteca del Congreso Nacional de Chile, *www.bcn.cl/guias/tribunales-de-familia* (accessed September 21, 2011).

8. Biosociality was originally introduced by Rabinow (2008) to work against sociobiological determinism and to theorize how new social relationships and

identities become possible with the creation of new biotechnical categories of suffering and human life.

9. While the advent of biomedical knowledge turned bodies into objects separate from the mind, individualized disease, and solidified notions of the embodied, individual self (see Lock and Nguyen 2010), Charcot and Freud initiated the objectification of the mind and human suffering through psychotherapy (Lock and Nguyen 2010).

10. Many have hailed the classification of habitual abuse, with its criminal implications, as an important innovation in the 2005 version of the Family Violence Law. However, a variety of problems have arisen with this classification, including, quite notably, judges' uncertainties in how to apply the classification because of the lack of specificity in the law. It is often up to judges to decide in practice how to apply this aspect of the law. This is crucially important, as cases of habitual abuse go to the public prosecutor while other sorts of abuse-related issues, including divorce, are seen in the family courts.

The Family Violence Law of 2005, unlike the 1994 version, no longer emphasizes reconciliation. Greatly expanded jail sentences, steep fines, long-term restraining orders, and other punishments are now highlighted, and the penalties are much stiffer (Franceschet 2008:13, 26). Cases are handled by the family court system or the public prosecutor, depending on the assessed severity of the abuse. The implementation of the family court system in Chile is part of the judicial system overhaul that took place in the early to mid-2000s, and this has implied many changes for women seeking help for domestic violence through the judicial system as well.

Chapter 4

1. A *MIRista* is a person who was involved with the MIR, the Movimiento de Izquierda Revolucionaria (Movement of the Revolutionary Left), an armed Marxist group that fought for class equality and workers' rights during the late 1960s, 1970s, and 1980s and exists in different forms into the present. Pinochet's dictatorship actively and consistently persecuted members and suspected members of the MIR.

2. Another woman I interviewed gave a similar analysis. "Workers have marches to protest terrible wages, she told me, and the authorities squelch their efforts at public participation . . . Still people abuse other people's rights. . . . Honestly, I don't feel like there's a one-hundred percent democracy here in Chile. There has been a change, but only up to a point. Because still . . . there are a lot of poor people in the country who continue to be poor."

3. Others have pointed out that neoliberal policies, ideologies, and practices are mobilized in diverse ways in specific contexts (Harvey 2007; Hodgson 2008; Ong 2006).

Chapter 5

1. This chapter heavily draws from Parson (2010b).
2. Han (2011) has documented a broad pattern of medicalization of distress produced by poverty, debt, and violence in the shifting political, economic, and discursive landscapes of the postdictatorship era in Chile.
3. See Gill (1994) for a cogent analysis of the ways in which upper-class women's feminine identities depend on their exploitation of lower-class women's domestic labor.
4. Petryna (2002) found that social ties of various sorts were important for victims of the Chernobyl disaster in the Ukraine being able to access support and, ultimately, biological citizenship under the newly formed post-Soviet government.
5. Material excerpted from the book *The Millionth Circle* © 1999 by Jean Shinoda Bolen, M.D. Red Wheeler/Weiser, LLC Newburyport, MA, and San Francisco, CA. *www.redwheelerweiser.com*
6. In a similar vein, Fassin and Rechtman (2009) have noted that the language of trauma and the ways this paradigm has been appropriated in modernist projects elide the *sources* of suffering in favor of a focus on cataloging symptoms through psychiatric nosologies, such as post-traumatic stress disorder (PTSD). In a parallel fashion, the language of women "victims" of domestic violence in Chile can be seen as a cultural form of avoiding an often-uncomfortable focus on the inequalities that produce and reproduce domestic violence against women and that contribute to normalizing that violence.
7. In a similar vein, Becker (1997:4) has observed that in the face of life-altering disruption, "Restoring order to life necessitates reworking understandings of the self and the world, redefining the disruption and life itself."

Chapter 6

1. A *cacerolazo* is a form of popular protest that involves beating pots and pans in the streets, last performed during the dictatorship.
2. Other posters asserted: "Women have the right to quality care," "For a participative municipal policy," "Less talking, more solutions," "Enough with empty words, more actions, more rights," "We demand a working group with women's participation," "Borough policy for more women's rights," "No more excuses! Solutions now!" and "More rights, more opportunities for women."
3. Observatorio Género y Equidad's website is *www.observatoriogeneroyliderazgo.cl.*

Chapter 7

1. See Farmer 2005.

Appendix 1

1. This question is phrased to avoid a "blame the victim" connotation (cf. Marchand-Arias 1998).

Works Cited

Abu-Lughod, Lila
    1991   Writing against Culture. In *Recapturing Anthropology*. R. G. Fox,
            ed. Pp. 137–62. Santa Fe, NM: School of American Research Press.
            Distributed by the University of Washington Press.
    2002   Do Muslim Women Really Need Saving?: Anthropological Reflec-
            tions on Cultural Relativism and Its Others. *American Anthropolo-*
            gist 104(3):783–90.
Adelman, Madelaine
    2004   The Battering State: Towards a Political Economy of Domestic
            Violence. *Journal of Poverty: Innovations on Social, Political & Eco-*
            nomic Inequalities 8(3):55–74.
Agamben, Giorgio
    1995   *Homo Sacer: Sovereign Power and Bare Life*. Stanford, CA: Stanford
            University Press.
    1999   The Witness. In *Remnants of Auschwitz: The Witness and the Ar-*
            chive. Trans. Daniel Heller-Roazen. Pp. 15–26. New York: Zone
            Books.
Agger, Inger, and Søren Buus Jensen
    1996   *Trauma and Healing under State Terrorism*. London: Zed Books.
Agosín, Marjorie
    2007   *Tapestries of Hope, Threads of Love: The Arpillera Movement in*
            Chile. Lanham, MD: Rowman and Littlefield.
Ahearn, Laura
    2001   Language and Agency. *Annual Review of Anthropology* 30:109–37.
Alcalde, M. Cristina
    2010   *The Woman in the Violence: Gender, Poverty and Resistance in Peru*.
            Nashville: Vanderbilt University Press.
Alvarez, Sonia E., Evelina Dagnino, and Arturo Escobar
    1998   *Cultures of Politics/Politics of Cultures: Re-Visioning Latin Ameri-*
            can Social Movements. Boulder, CO: Westview.

Anderson, Benedict
1998   *Imagined Communities*. London: Verso.
Basu, Srimati
2012   Judges of Normality: Mediating Marriage in the Family Courts of Kolkata, India. *Signs* 37(2):469–92.
Beauvoir, Simone de
1965   *The Second Sex*. New York: Bantam Books.
Becker, Gaylene
1997   *Disrupted Lives: How People Create Meaning in a Chaotic World.* Berkeley: University of California Press.
Behar, Ruth
1996   *The Vulnerable Observer: Anthropology That Breaks Your Heart.* Boston: Beacon.
Behar, Ruth, and Deborah A. Gordon
1995   *Women Writing Culture*. Berkeley: University of California Press.
Beltrán-Martínez, M.
2007   Mecanismo de seguimiento de la Convención de Belém do Pará (MESECVI). Presented at Reunión OPS Valid. Leyes Viol., Washington, DC.
Bernard, H. Russell
1995   *Research Methods in Anthropology: Qualitative and Quantitative Approaches*. 2nd edition. Thousand Oaks, CA: Sage.
Biehl, João Guilherme
2005   *Vita: Life in a Zone of Social Abandonment.* Berkeley: University of California Press.
2007   *Will to Live: AIDS Therapies and the Politics of Survival*. Princeton, NJ: Princeton University Press.
Biehl, João Guilherme, Byron Good, and Arthur Kleinman
2007   *Subjectivity: Ethnographic Investigations.* Berkeley: University of California Press.
Bolen, Jean Shinoda
1999   *The Millionth Circle: How to Change Ourselves and the World; The Essential Guide to Women's Circles.* Berkeley, CA: Conari Press.
Bourdieu, Pierre
1990 [1980]   *The Logic of Practice.* Richard Nice, trans. Stanford, CA: Stanford University Press.
2001 [1998]   *Masculine Domination.* Richard Nice, trans. Stanford, CA: Stanford University Press.
Bourdieu, Pierre, and Loïc Waquant
1992   *An Invitation to Reflexive Sociology.* Chicago: University of Chicago Press.

Bourgois, Philippe
    2009   Recognizing Invisible Violence: A Thirty-Year Ethnographic Retrospective. In *Global Health in Times of Violence*. Barbara Rylko-Bauer, Linda Whiteford, and Paul Farmer, eds. Pp. 17–40. Santa Fe, NM: School for Advanced Research Press.
Brettell, Caroline
    2003   *Anthropology and Migration: Essays on Transnationalism, Ethnicity, and Identity*. Walnut Creek, CA: AltaMira.
Bumiller, Kristin
    2008   *In an Abusive State: How Neoliberalism Appropriated the Feminist Movement against Sexual Violence*. Durham, NC: Duke University Press.
Bunch, Charlotte, and Roxanna Carrillo
    1991   *Gender Violence: A Development and Human Rights Issue*. Highland Park, NJ: Plowshares Press.
Bunster-Burotto, Ximena
    1986   Surviving beyond Fear: Women and Torture in Latin America. In *Women and Change in Latin America*. J. Nash and H. Safa, eds. Pp. 297–325. South Hadley, MA: Bergin and Garvey.
Caldeira, Teresa P. R., and James Holston
    1999   Democracy and Violence in Brazil. *Comparative Studies in Society and History* 41(4):691–729.
Carabineros de Chile
    1999   Boletín de instrucciones de Carabineros de Chile. No. 478. Santiago, Chile.
Carrillo, Roxanna, Charlotte Bunch, and Rima Shore
    1998   Violence against Women. In *Women in the Third World: An Encyclopedia of Contemporary Issues*. Nelly P. Stromquist, ed. Pp. 59–68. New York: Garland.
Casas, Lidia, Claudia Dides, and Soledad Pérez
    2001   *Sistematización de información sobre control de medidas y sanciones, en virtud del artículo 5 de La Ley 19.325 de Violencia Intrafamiliar y de estudio cualitativo sobre percepción de demandantes sobre efectividad de la misma ley*. Santiago, Chile: SERNAM.
Ceballo, Rosario, Cynthia Ramirez, Marcelo Castillo, Gabriela Alejandra Caballero, and Betsy Lozoff
    2004   Domestic Violence and Women's Mental Health in Chile. *Psychology of Women Quarterly* 28(4):298–308.
Chavez, Leo R.
    2008   *The Latino Threat: Constructing Immigrants, Citizens, and the Nation*. Stanford, CA: Stanford University Press.

Chen, Ping-Hsin, Sue Rovi, Marielos Vega, Abbie Jacobs, and Mark S. Johnson
    2009   Relation of Domestic Violence to Health Status among Hispanic
        Women. *Journal of Health Care for the Poor and Underserved*
        20:569–82.
Chuchryk, Patricia M.
    1989   Subversive Mothers: The Women's Opposition to the Military Re-
        gime in Chile. In *Women, the State, and Development.* S. E. Charl-
        ton and J. Everett, eds. Pp. 130–51. New York: State University of
        New York Press.
Clifford, James, George E. Marcus, and School of American Research
    1986   *Writing Culture: The Poetics and Politics of Ethnography.* A School
        of American Research Advanced Seminar. Berkeley: University of
        California Press.
Coker, Ann L., Keith E. Davis, Ileana Arias, Sujata Desai, Maureen Sanderson,
    Heather M. Brandt, and Paige H. Smith
    2002   Physical and Mental Health Effects of Intimate Partner Violence
        for Men and Women. *American Journal of Preventive Medicine*
        23(4):260–68.
Comisión Chilena de Derechos Humanos, and Fundación Ideas
    1999   *Nunca más en Chile: Sintesis corregida y actualizada del informe
        Rettig.* 2nd edition. Santiago: LOM ediciones.
Corporación Humanas
    2008   *Quinta Encuesta Nacional "Percepciones de las mujeres sobre su
        situación y condiciones de vida en Chile."* Santiago, Chile: Corpo-
        ración Humanas.
Counts, Dorothy, Judith Brown, and Jaquelyn Campbell
    1992   *Sanctions and Sanctuary: Cultural Perspectives on the Beating of
        Wives.* Boulder: Westview Press.
Csordas, Thomas J.
    1990   Embodiment as a Paradigm for Anthropology. *Ethos* 18(1):5–47.
Dandavati, Annie G.
    2005   *Engendering Democracy in Chile.* New York: Peter Lang.
Das, Veena
    1995   *Critical Events: An Anthropological Perspective on Contemporary
        India.* New York: Oxford University Press.
    2000   The Act of Witnessing: Violence, Poisonous Knowledge, and Sub-
        jectivity. In *Violence and Subjectivity.* V. Das, A. Kleinman, M.
        Ramphele, and P. Reynolds, eds. Pp. 205–25. Berkeley: University
        of California Press.
    2001   *Remaking a World: Violence, Social Suffering, and Recovery.* Berke-
        ley: University of California Press.
    2008   Violence, Gender, and Subjectivity. *Annual Review of Anthro-
        pology* 37:283–99.

Das, Veena, and Ranendra K. Das
2007 How the Body Speaks: Illness and the Lifeworld among the Urban Poor. In *Subjectivity: Ethnographic Investigations.* J. Biehl, B. Good, and A. Kleinman, eds. Pp. 66–97. Berkeley: University of California Press.
Das, Veena, and Arthur Kleinman
2001 Introduction. In *Remaking a World: Violence, Social Suffering, and Recovery.* V. Das, A. Kleinman, M. Lock, M. Ramphele, and P. Reynolds, eds. Pp. 1–30. Berkeley: University of California Press.
Das, Veena, and Deborah Poole
2004 *Anthropology in the Margins of the State.* Santa Fe, NM: School of American Research Press.
DelVecchio Good, Mary-Jo
2007 The Biotechnical Embrace and the Medical Imaginary. In *Subjectivity: Ethnographic Investigations.* J. Biehl, B. Good, and A. Kleinman, eds. Pp. 362–80. Berkeley: University of California Press.
DelVecchio Good, Mary-Jo, and Byron J. Good
1988 Ritual, the State, and the Transformation of Emotional Discourse in Iranian Society. *Culture, Medicine and Psychiatry* 12(1):43–63.
Dorfman, Ariel
2002 *Exorcising Terror: The Incredible Unending Trial of General Augusto Pinochet.* New York: Seven Stories Press.
Egert, Ana María
2002 Depresión Masoquista: La Vocación De Sufrir. *Revista Ya* (magazine of *El Mercurio*), May 11: 1–2. Santiago, Chile.
El Agua Consultores Asociados
1997 *Informe final: estudio sobre la aplicación de la ley 19.325 y la formulación de propuestas para mejorar su eficiencia y eficacia.* Santiago, Chile: SERNAM.
Enloe, Cynthia H.
1983 *Does Khaki Become You?: The Militarization of Women's Lives.* Boston: South End Press.
2000 *Maneuvers.* Berkeley: University of California Press.
Farmer, Paul
2005 *Pathologies of Power: Health, Human Rights, and the New War on the Poor.* Berkeley: University of California Press.
Fassin, Didier, and Richard Rechtman
2009 *The Empire of Trauma: An Inquiry into the Condition of Victimhood.* Princeton, NJ: Princeton University Press.
Foucault, Michel
1979 *Discipline and Punish: The Birth of a Prison.* London: Peregrine Books.

Foucault, Michel, and Colin Gordon
  1980   *Power/Knowledge: Selected Interviews and Other Writings, 1972–1977.* Brighton, UK: Harvester Press.
Franceschet, Susan
  2008   The Politics of Domestic Violence Policy in Latin America. Institute for Advanced Policy Research Technical Paper Series Technical Paper No. TP-08001. University of Calgary, Alberta, Canada.
Fries, Lorena, and Verónica Matus
  1999   *El derecho: Trama y conjura patriarcal.* Santiago, Chile: LOM ediciones.
García-Moreno, Claudia
  2006   World Health Organization Multi-Country Study on Violence against Women. Geneva, Switzerland: World Health Organization.
Gaviola, Edda, Eliana Largo, and Sandra Palestro
  1994   *Una historia necesaria: Mujeres en Chile 1973–1990.* Santiago, Chile: Akí & Aora.
Geertz, Clifford
  1973   *The Interpretation of Cultures: Selected Essays.* New York: Basic Books.
  2000   *Available Light: Anthropological Reflections on Philosophical Topics.* Princeton, NJ: Princeton University Press.
Geis, Irene
  1989   *Pluma and Pincel,* 8 March 1989: 13
Gill, Lesley
  1994   *Precarious Dependencies.* New York: Columbia University Press.
  2004   *The School of the Americas: Military Training and Political Violence in the Americas.* Durham, NC: Duke University Press.
Glick, Peter, Susan T. Fiske, Antonio Mladinic, Jose L. Saiz, Dominic Abrams, Barbara Masser, Bolanle Adetoun, et al.
  2000   Beyond Prejudice as Simple Antipathy: Hostile and Benevolent Sexism across Cultures. *Journal of Personality and Social Psychology* 79(5):763–75.
Gobierno de Chile
  1994   Ley de Violencia Intrafamiliar. Santiago, Chile: Ediciones Publiley.
  2004   Ley de Matrimonio Civil (Ley 19.947).
  2005a   Historia de la Ley N° 20.066 establece Ley de Violencia Intrafamiliar. Biblioteca del Congreso Nacional de Chile.
  2005b   Informe Comisión Valech. Santiago, Chile.
Goldstein, Daniel M.
  2004   *The Spectacular City: Violence and Performance in Urban Bolivia.* Durham, NC: Duke University Press.

Gómez-Barris, Macarena
   2009   *Where Memory Dwells: Culture and State Violence in Chile.* Berke-
           ley: University of California Press.
Gordon, Deborah
   1988   Writing Culture, Writing Feminism: The Poetics and Politics of Ex-
           perimental Ethnography. *Inscriptions* 3(4):7–26.
Green, Linda
   1999   *Fear as a Way of Life: Mayan Widows in Rural Guatemala.* New
           York: Columbia University Press.
Guarnaccia, Peter, Roberto Lewis-Fernández, and Melissa Rivera Marano
   2003   Toward a Puerto Rican Popular Nosology: Nervios and Ataque de
           Nervios. *Culture, Medicine and Psychiatry* 27(3):339–66.
Guillaudat, Patrick, and Pierre Mouterde
   1998   *Los movimientos sociales en Chile 1973–1993.* Santiago, Chile:
           LOM ediciones.
Hacking, Ian
   1998   *Mad Travelers: Reflections on the Reality of Transient Mental Ill-
           nesses.* Charlottesville, VA: University Press of Virginia.
Han, Clara
   2011   Symptoms of Another Life: Time, Possibility, and Domestic
           Relations in Chile's Credit Economy. *Cultural Anthropology*
           26(1):7–32.
Harvey, David
   2007   *A Brief History of Neoliberalism.* New York: Oxford University Press.
Hautzinger, Sarah J.
   2007   *Violence in the City of Women: Police and Batterers in Bahia, Bra-
           zil.* Berkeley: University of California Press.
Hayner, Priscilla
   2001   *Unspeakable Truths: Confronting State Terror and Atrocity.* New
           York: Routledge.
Held, Virginia
   2006   *The Ethics of Care: Personal, Political and Global.* Oxford: Oxford
           University Press.
Herman, Judith Lewis
   1992   *Trauma and Recovery.* New York: Basic Books.
Hidalgo, Paulina
   2003   Como "campaña del terror" califican spots contra el divorcio de la
           Iglesia Católica. *La Nacion,* 25 September 2003: 12.
Hodgson, Dorothy Louise
   1995   "My Daughter . . . Belongs to the Government Now": Marriage,
           Maasai, and the Tanzanian State. *Canadian Journal of African
           Studies* 30(1):106–23.

2008   Cosmopolitics, Neoliberalism, and the State: The Indigenous Rights Movement in Africa. In *Anthropology and the New Cosmopolitanism: Rooted, Feminist, and Vernacular Perspectives*. P. Werbner, ed. Pp. 215–30. New York: Berg.

Htun, Mala
2003   *Sex and the State: Abortion, Divorce, and the Family under Latin American Dictatorships and Democracies*. New York: Cambridge University Press.

Jackson, Michael
1998   *Minima Ethnographica: Intersubjectivity and the Anthropological Project*. Chicago: University of Chicago Press.

Jaquette, Jane S.
1989   *The Women's Movement in Latin America: Feminism and the Transition to Democracy*. Boston: Unwin Hyman.

Jenkins, Janis Hunter
1991   The State Construction of Affect: Political Ethos and Mental Health among Salvadoran Refugees. *Culture, Medicine and Psychiatry* 15(2):139–65.
1996   The Impress of Extremity: Women's Experience of Trauma and Political Violence. In *Gender and Health: An International Perspective*. C. F. Sargent and C. Brettell, eds. Pp. 278–91. Upper Saddle River, NJ: Prentice Hall.

Johnson, Janet Elise
2009   *Gender Violence in Russia: The Politics of Feminist Intervention*. Bloomington: Indiana University Press.

Kaplan, Temma
2004.   *Taking Back the Streets: Women, Youth, and Direct Democracy*. Berkeley: University of California Press.

Kirmayer, Laurence
2007   Failures of Imagination: The Refugee's Predicament. In *Understanding Trauma: Integrating Biological, Clinical, and Cultural Perspectives*. L. Kirmayer, R. Lemelson, and M. Barad, eds. Pp. 363–81. Cambridge: Cambridge University Press.

Kleinman, Arthur
1988   *The Illness Narratives: Suffering, Healing, and the Human Condition*. New York: Basic Books.
1995   *Writing at the Margin: Discourse between Anthropology and Medicine*. Berkeley: University of California Press.
1999   Experience and Its Moral Modes: Culture, Human Conditions, and Disorder. *Tanner Lectures on Human Values* 20:355–420.

Kleinman, Arthur, Veena Das, and Margaret Lock
1997a   Introduction. In *Social Suffering*. A. Kleinman, V. Das, and M. Lock, eds. Pp. ix–xxvii. Berkeley: University of California Press.

Kleinman, Arthur, Veena Das, and Margaret M. Lock, eds.
1997b   *Social Suffering.* Berkeley: University of California Press.
Kleinman, Arthur, and Joan Kleinman
1997   The Appeal of Experience; the Dismay of Images: Cultural Appro-
         priations of Suffering in Our Times. In *Social Suffering.* A. Klein-
         man, V. Das, and M. Lock, eds. Pp. 1–24. Berkeley: University of
         California.
Kwiatkowski, Lynn
2011   Prolonging Suffering: Domestic Violence, Political Economy, and
         the State in Northern Vietnam. Working Paper 299 *Gendered Per-
         spectives in International Development.* East Lansing, MI: Center
         for Gender in Global Context, Michigan State University.
Lamb, Sarah
2001   Being a Widow and Other Life Stories: The Interplay between
         Lives and Words. *Anthropology and Humanism* 26(1):16–34.
Lamphere, Louise, Helena Ragoné, and Patricia Zavella
1997   *Situated Lives: Gender and Culture in Everyday Life.* New York:
         Routledge.
Larraín, Soledad
1994   *Violencia puertas adentro: La mujer golpeada.* Santiago, Chile: Edi-
         torial Universitaria.
Lazarus-Black, Mindie
2007   *Everyday Harm: Domestic Violence, Court Rites, and Cultures of
         Reconciliation.* Urbana: University of Illinois Press.
Levinson, David
1989   *Family Violence in Cross-Cultural Perspective.* Newbury Park, CA:
         Sage.
Lincoln, Yvonna S., and Egon G. Guba
1985   *Naturalistic Inquiry.* Newbury Park, CA: Sage.
Lock, Margaret
2008   The Tempering of Medical Anthropology: Troubling Natural Cate-
         gories. *Medical Anthropology Quarterly* 15(4):478–92.
Lock, Margaret M., and Vinh-Kim Nguyen
2010   *An Anthropology of Biomedicine.* Chichester, UK: Wiley-Blackwell.
Loveman, Brian, and Elizabeth Lira
2002   *El espejismo de la reconciliación política: Chile 1990–2002.* San-
         tiago, Chile: LOM.
Luborsky, Mark
1994   The Retirement Process: Making the Person and Cultural Mean-
         ings Malleable. *Medical Anthropology Quarterly* 8(4):411–29.
Lúnecken Reyes, Graciela Alejandra
2000   *Violencia política (violencia política en Chile, 1983–1986).* San-
         tiago, Chile: Arzobispado de Santiago.

Marchand-Arias, Rosa E.
1998   *Battered Women's Sheltered Lives: An Exercise in "Feminist" Eth-nography.* PhD dissertation, Department of Anthropology, University of Michigan.

Martínez, Valentina
2009   *Entre territorios y sentidos: Evaluación de atención en violencia hacia la mujer en la atención primaria de salud.* Centro Clínico y de Investigación Corporación La Morada UNFPA.

Maynes, Mary Jo, Jennifer L. Pierce, and Barbara Laslett
2008   *Telling Stories: The Use of Personal Narratives in the Social Sciences and History.* Ithaca, NY: Cornell University Press.

Mechanic, Mindy B., Tern L. Weaver, and Patricia A. Resick
2008   Mental Health Consequences of Intimate Partner Abuse: A Multidimensional Assessment of Four Different Forms of Abuse. *Violence Against Women* 14:634–54.

Menjívar, Cecilia
2011   *Enduring Violence: Ladina Women's Lives in Guatemala.* Berkeley: University of California Press.

Merry, Sally Engle
2000   *Colonizing Hawai'i: The Cultural Power of Law.* Princeton, NJ: Princeton University Press.
2001   Spatial Governmentality and the New Urban Social Order: Controlling Gender Violence through Law. *American Anthropologist* 103(1):16–29.
2006   *Human Rights and Gender Violence: Translating International Law into Local Justice.* Chicago: University of Chicago Press.
2009   *Gender Violence: A Cultural Perspective.* Oxford: Wiley-Blackwell.
2011   Measuring the World: Indicators, Human Rights, and Global Governance. *Current Anthropology* 52 (suppl. 3):S83–S95.

Metzl, Jonathan M., and Anna Kirkland, eds.
2011   *Against Health: How Health Became the New Morality.* New York: New York University Press.

Mintz, Sidney Wilfred
1960   *Worker in the Cane: A Puerto Rican Life History.* New Haven: Yale University Press.

Mohanty, Chandra Talpade
1991   Cartographies of Struggle: Third World Women and the Politics of Feminism. In *Third World Women and the Politics of Feminism.* C T. Mohanty, A. Russo, and L. Torres, eds. Pp. 1–50. Bloomington: Indiana University Press.

Molé, Noelle
2011   *Labor Disorders in Neoliberal Italy: Mobbing, Well-Being and the Workplace.* Bloomington: Indiana University Press.

Moltedo, Cecilia
 1999   *Campaña de las agencias de las Naciones Unidas en Latinoamerica
         y el Caribe por los derechos humanos de la mujer: Informe nacional
         sobre la situación de la violencia de género contra las mujeres en
         Chile.* United Nations Development Programme. Santiago, Chile:
         Consultora PNUD.
Montecino, Sonia, and María Elena Acuña, eds.
 1996   *Diálogos sobre el género masculino en Chile.* Santiago, Chile: Bravo
         y Allende Editores.
Montecino Aguirre, Sonia, and Josefina Rossetti, eds.
 1990   *Tramas para un nuevo destino: Propuestas de la concertación de mu-
         jeres por la democracia.* Santiago, Chile: Arancibia Hnos.
Moore, Henrietta L.
 1988   *Feminism and Anthropology.* Cambridge: Polity Press.
 1994   *A Passion for Difference: Essays in Anthropology and Gender.*
         Bloomington: Indiana University Press.
Morales, Leonidas
 2000   *Cartas de petición: Chile 1973–1989.* Santiago, Chile: Editorial
         Planeta Chilena.
Mullings, Leith
 2006   Resistance and Resilience, the Sojourner Syndrome and the
         Social Context of Reproduction in Central Harlem. In *Gender,
         Race, Class, and Health: Intersectional Approaches.* 1st edition.
         A. J. Schulz and L. Mullings, eds. Pp. 345–70. San Francisco:
         Jossey-Bass.
Murthy, Rangaswamy Srinivasa, ed.
 2001   *The World Health Report 2001. Mental Health: New Understand-
         ing, New Hope.* Geneva, Switzerland: World Health Organization.
Olavarría, José
 2001a   *¿Hombres a la deriva?* Santiago, Chile: FLACSO-Chile.
Olavarría, José, ed.
 2001b   *Hombres: Identidad/es y violencia.* Santiago, Chile:
         FLACSO-Chile.
Olavarría, José, and Enrique Moletto, eds.
 2002   *Hombres: Identidades y sexualidad/es.* Santiago, Chile:
         FLACSO-Chile.
Ong, Aihwa
 2006   *Neoliberalism as Exception: Mutations in Citizenship and Sover-
         eignty.* Durham, NC: Duke University Press.
Organisation for Economic Co-operation and Development
 2011   *Society at a Glance 2011: OECD Social Indicators.* Paris: Organisa-
         tion for Economic Co-operation and Development. Available at
         www.oecd.org/els/social/indicators/SAG.

Ortner, Sherry B.
    1996   *Making Gender: The Politics and Erotics of Culture.* Boston:
            Beacon.
Padín, Betsabe
    2001   *Relatos, rupturas y saberes: Taller historias de vida.* Santiago, Chile:
            Instituto de la Mujer.
Paley, Julia
    2001   *Marketing Democracy: Power and Social Movements in Post-Dicta-
            torship Chile.* Berkeley: University of California Press.
Parson, Nia
    2005   *Gendered Suffering and Social Transformations: Domestic Violence,
            Dictatorship and Democracy in Chile.* PhD Dissertation, Depart-
            ment of Anthropology, Rutgers University, New Brunswick, NJ.
    2010a   "I Am Not [Just] a Rabbit Who Has a Bunch of Children!": Agency
            in the Midst of Suffering at the Intersections of Global Inequali-
            ties, Gendered Violence, and Migration. *Violence Against Women*
            16(8):881–901.
    2010b   Transformative Ties: Gendered Violence, Forms of Recovery, and
            Shifting Subjectivities in Chile. *Medical Anthropology Quarterly*
            24(1):64–84.
    2012   "Single Women Are Bitter": The Gendered Production of Affective
            States in Chile. In *Gender in Cross-Cultural Perspective.* 6th ed. C.
            B. Brettell and C. F. Sargent, eds. Pp. 263–71. Upper Saddle River,
            NJ: Prentice Hall.
    Forthcoming   Health at the Intersections of Undocumented Status and Gen-
            der Based Partner Violence. *Violence Against Women.*
Personal Narratives Group, ed.
    1989   *Interpreting Women's Lives: Feminist Theory and Personal Narra-
            tives.* Bloomington: Indiana University Press.
Petryna, Adriana
    2002   *Life Exposed: Biological Citizens after Chernobyl.* Princeton, NJ:
            Princeton University Press.
Pietikäinen, Petteri
    2007   *Neurosis and Modernity: The Age of Nervousness in Sweden.* Leiden:
            Brill.
Plesset, Sonja
    2006   *Sheltering Women: Negotiating Gender and Violence in Northern
            Italy.* Stanford, CA: Stanford University Press.
Power, Margaret
    2002   *Right-Wing Women in Chile: Feminine Power and the Struggle
            against Allende, 1964–1973.* University Park: Pennsylvania State
            University Press.

Quiroz, Carmen Gloria
    1991   El machismo y la violencia intrafamiliar. In *Modelos teóricos y metodológicos de intervención en violencia doméstica y sexual.* A. Cáceres and V. Mártinez, eds. Pp. 11–15. Santiago, Chile: Casa de la Mujer La Morada.
Rabinow, Paul
    2008   Artificiality and Enlightenment: From Sociobiology to Biosociality. In *Anthropologies of Modernity: Foucault, Governmentality, and Life Politics.* J. X. Inda, ed. Pp. 181–93. Oxford: Blackwell.
Rapp, Rayna
    1999   *Testing Women, Testing the Fetus: The Social Impact of Amniocentesis in America.* New York: Routledge.
Reed-Danahay, Deborah
    2005   *Locating Bourdieu.* Bloomington, IN: Indiana University Press.
Renzetti, Claire M., Jeffrey L. Edleson, and Raquel Kennedy Bergen
    2001   *The Sourcebook on Violence against Women.* Thousand Oaks, CA: Sage.
Rettig, Raul Guissen
    1993   *Report of the Chilean National Commission on Truth and Reconciliation.* Vols. 1–2. Notre Dame, IN: Center for Civil and Human Rights, Notre Dame Law School.
Richards, Patricia
    2004   *Pobladoras, Indígenas, and the State: Conflicts over Women's Rights in Chile.* New Brunswick, NJ: Rutgers University Press.
Rojas, Paz, María Inés Muñoz, María Luisa Ortiz, and Viviana Uribe
    2002   *Todas ibamos a ser reinas.* Santiago, Chile: LOM ediciones.
Rylko-Bauer, Barbara, and Paul Farmer
    2002   Managed Care or Managed Inequality?: A Call for Critiques of Market-Based Medicine. *Medical Anthropology Quarterly* 16(4):476–502.
Sanford, Victoria, and Asale Angel-Ajani
    2006   *Engaged Observer: Anthropology, Advocacy, and Activism.* New Brunswick, NJ: Rutgers University Press.
Sargent, Carolyn, and Grace Bascope
    1996   Ways of Knowing about Birth in Three Cultures. *Medical Anthropology Quarterly* 10(2):213–36.
Scarry, Elaine
    1985   *The Body in Pain: The Making and Unmaking of the World.* New York: Oxford University Press.
Scheper-Hughes, Nancy
    1992   *Death without Weeping: The Violence of Everyday Life in Brazil.* Berkeley: University of California Press.

Scheper-Hughes, Nancy, and Philippe I. Bourgois, eds.
2004   *Violence in War and Peace.* Malden, MA: Blackwell.
Scheper-Hughes, Nancy, and Margaret M. Lock
1987   The Mindful Body: A Prolegomenon to Future Work in Medical Anthropology. *Medical Anthropology Quarterly* 1(1):6–41.
SERNAM
2002   *Detección y análisis de la prevalencia de la violencia intrafamiliar.* Santiago, Chile: SERNAM.
2004a   *Mujeres Chilenas: Tendencias en la última década censos 1992–2002.* Santiago, Chile: SERNAM.
2004b   Denuncias por violencia intrafamiliar triplican las de robo con violencia: Conmemoran 10 años de Ley De Violencia Intrafamiliar. Press release. Santiago, Chile: SERNAM.
2011   *Taller 5 enfrentándonos al mundo laboral.* Santiago, Chile: SERNAM.
SERNAM, DOMOS, and LA MORADA
2007   *Análisis y evaluación de la ruta crítica en mujeres afectadas por violencia en la relación de pareja.* Documento de Trabajo 107. Santiago, Chile: SERNAM.
Stacey, Judith
1988   Can There Be a Feminist Ethnography? *Women's Studies International Forum* 11(1):21–27.
Stark, Evan
2007   *Coercive Control: The Entrapment of Women in Personal Life.* Oxford: Oxford University Press.
Stern, Steve
2004   *Remembering Pinochet's Chile: On the Eve of London, 1998.* Durham, NC: Duke University Press.
2006   *Battling for Hearts and Minds: Memory Struggles in Pinochet's Chile, 1973–1988.* Durham, NC: Duke University Press.
2010   *Reckoning with Pinochet: The Memory Question in Democratic Chile, 1989–2006.* Durham, NC: Duke University Press.
Ticktin, Miriam
2011   *Casualties of Care: Immigration and the Politics of Humanitarianism in France.* Berkeley: University of California Press.
Trumper, Ricardo, and Patricia Tomic
1998   From a Cancerous Body to a Reconciled Family: Legitimizing Neoliberalism in Chile. In *Transgressing Borders: Critical Perspectives on Gender, Household, and Culture.* S. Ilcan and L. Phillips, eds. Pp. 3–18. Westport, CT: Bergin & Garvey.
Tsing, Anna Lowenhaupt
2005   *Friction: An Ethnography of Global Connection.* Princeton, NJ: Princeton University Press.

Turshen, Meredeth
  2000   The Political Economy of Violence against Women During Armed
          Conflict in Uganda. *Social Research* 67(3):803–24.
  2007   *Women's Health Movements: A Global Force for Change*. New York:
          Palgrave Macmillan.
Valdés, Teresa
  1991   Being Female and Poor: A Double Oppression. In *Popular Culture
          in Chile: Resistance and Survival*. K. Aman and C. Parker, eds. Pp.
          97–106. Boulder, CO: Westview.
Valdés, Teresa, Marisa Weinstein, María Isabel Toledo, and Lilian Letelier
  1989   Centros de Madres 1973–1990 ¿Sólo Disciplinamiento? Docu-
          mento de trabajo 416. Latin American Social Sciences Institute
          (FLASCO), Santiago, Chile.
Valenzuela, María Elena
  1998   Women and the Democratization Process in Chile. In *Women and
          Democracy: Latin America and Central and Eastern Europe*. J. S.
          Jaquette and S. L. Wolchik, eds. Pp. 47–74. Baltimore: Johns Hop-
          kins University Press.
Wheatley, Elizabeth
  1994   How Can We Engender Ethnography with a Feminist Imagination?
          A Rejoinder to Judith Stacey. *Women's Studies International Forum*
          17(4):403–16.
Wies, Jennifer R., and Hillary J. Haldane, eds.
  2011   *Anthropology at the Front Lines of Gender-Based Violence*. Nash-
          ville, TN: Vanderbilt University Press.
Willen, Sarah S.
  2011   Do "Illegal" Migrants Have a Right to Health? Engaging Ethical
          Theory as Social Practice at a Tel Aviv Open Clinic. *Medical An-
          thropology Quarterly* 25(3):303–30.
Winn, Peter
  1986   *Weavers of Revolution: The Yarur Workers and Chile's Road to So-
          cialism*. New York: Oxford University Press.
Young, Allan
  1995   *The Harmony of Illusions: Inventing Post-Traumatic Stress Disorder*.
          Princeton, NJ: Princeton University Press.
  1997   Suffering and the Origins of Traumatic Memory. In *Social Suffer-
          ing*. A. Kleinman, V. Das, and M. Lock, eds. Pp. 245–60. Berkeley:
          University of California Press.

Index

Page numbers in bold refer to illustrations